Illustrated

CHEVROLET

BUYER'S GUIDE™

Covers 1946–72
Stylemaster, Chevelle, Bel Air, Impala, Corvair, Fleetline and more

John Gunnell

Motorbooks International
Publishers & Wholesalers ®

First published in 1989 by Motorbooks
International Publishers & Wholesalers Inc, P O
Box 2, 729 Prospect Avenue, Osceola, WI 54020
USA

Motorbooks International is a certified
trademark, registered with the United States
Patent Office

Printed and bound in the United States of
America

The information in this book is true and
complete to the best of our knowledge. All
recommendations are made without any
guarantee on the part of the author or
publisher, who also disclaim any liability
incurred in connection with the use of this data
or specific details

We recognize that some words, model names
and designations, for example, mentioned
herein are the property of the trademark
holder. We use them for identification purposes
only. This is not an official publication

Library of Congress Cataloging-in-Publication Data
Gunnell, John
    Illustrated Chevrolet buyer's guide / John Gunnell.
      p. cm.
    ISBN 0-87938-317-8
    1. Chevrolet automobile—Purchasing. I. Title.
  TL215.C5G86   1989   89-3232
  629.2'222—dc19   CIP

On the front cover: The rare 1956 Chevrolet
Bel Air dual quad owned by Dave Boyd of
Dallas, Texas. *Jerry Heasley*
On the back cover: Chevy muscle! The 1966
Chevelle Super Sport 396 with simulated hood
scoops and recessed rear window.

This book is dedicated to my mother, Ceil
Gunnell, who spent many Wednesday after-
noons driving her son around the streets of
Staten Island, New York, to check out vintage cars in back yards, driveways and rick-
ety old garages. The enthusiasm she encour-
aged has lasted many years.

Contents

Acknowledgments

I would like to recognize the following individuals who contributed their knowledge of Chevrolet product history:

Robert C. Ackerson; Bruce Berghoff; Terry V. Boyce; Kenneth Buttolph; Jim Carlson; Pat Chappell; Bob Chauvin; Linda Clark; George H. Dammann; Gary Esse; Phil Hall; Robert Hensel; Tony Hossain; Ralph J. Kramer; Ed Lechtzin; Ray Miller; Doug Moorhead; "Pinky" Randall; Wally Rank; O.B. Smith; Robert Snowden; Tim Streblow; Larry Wallie; and Wes Yokum.

Additional thanks go to the many enthusiasts who own the cars that were photographed at car shows in Iola, Milwaukee, Jefferson, Elkhorn and Eagle River, Wisconsin, and Carlisle, Pennsylvania. Where possible, car owners have been identified in photo captions. Additional help with photos came from Mike Carbonella; Bill and Mary Mason; Chevrolet Motor Division; and Tim Streblow.

Comments and photo contributions are invited relating to any cars pictured in this book that might vary from original equipment specifications, which is always a possibility when taking photographs at collector car shows. Every effort will be made to incorporate improvements in future editions of *Illustrated Chevrolet Buyer's Guide*.

Preface

In 1987, I helped *Old Cars Weekly* organize a special exhibit at the Iola, Wisconsin, old-car show to celebrate Chevrolet's seventy-fifth anniversary. The goal was to display one Chevrolet car or truck for each year the company produced vehicles.

Postwar Chevys proved easy to attract; many fine cars made from 1946 to 1972 showed up. This seemed to prove that collecting Chevrolets is oriented toward postwar cars.

My own involvement with the collector car hobby started with postwar Chevrolets. My first collector car was a 1954 210 sedan, which I purchased because it reminded me of the 1955 Chevy Del Ray coupe that my grandfather gave me in 1965. Both cars were green and white. The first introduced me to driving; the second introduced me to the old-car hobby.

There have been other Chevys, both antique and late-model, in my life. One was a 1954 Handyman station wagon. Another was a 1953 210 two-door sedan, purchased as a parts car. My current family car is a 1980 Caprice Classic, one of the finest cars I have ever owned. Then there's the 1984 Camaro Z-28 with T-top and the five-liter engine, which I drive to work when I'm not using my antique cars.

While my Chevy enthusiasm isn't as widely known as a certain other personal marque loyalty, it's been part of my automotive experience since the beginning—and probably always will be. But I'll try not to let it get in the way of compiling an unbiased buyer's guide.

John Gunnell

Introduction

Once upon a time, the old-car hobby was basically a rich man's playground. Then, in the early 1950s the Model A Ford grew old enough to become collectible. Pretty soon, thousands of Americans were getting involved with restoring old cars.

As the fifties became the sixties, changes in the hobby took place. Cars made after World War Two started to fall into the antique category and become collectible. As this took place, the number of Chevys being collected increased dramatically.

Very much like what happened earlier with Model As, a cottage industry sprung up to supply the Chevy buffs with parts and information. New clubs were formed. Books about Chevrolets were published and found thousands of buyers. In short, the postwar Chevy became the king of the old-car world.

Younger collectors realized that some Chevys of the sixties and seventies were very special or rare. Collecting Corvairs and Corvettes became a big branch of the Chevrolet movement. Before long, late-model Novas, Chevelles and Camaros were being restored and entered in car shows. Enthusiast organizations evolved for Cosworth Vegas, Impalas and Super Sports.

This book isn't about any particular type of postwar Chevrolet. In fact, it's an attempt to survey all of them made between 1946 and 1972 that are—or promise to become—collectible. All but Corvettes and Camaros, that is.

Motorbooks International has already published separate buyer's guides for Corvettes and Camaros. This is fortunate, since both of these models deserve close inspection. You'll want to read the other books if 'vettes or Camaros are included in your Chevy fleet.

Now that we've covered the scope of this book, let's get into the organization and type of material included. First, the book is divided into six main sections. Within each section, Chevys with year-to-year similarities are grouped by model years. For example, the popular 1955-57 models make up one chapter.

At the beginning of each chapter, you'll find a table that rates the relative collectibility of different models with one to five stars. The more stars, the more collectible the model is. These ratings are subjective, however, and designed to show at a glance my top investment picks; that is, my educated guesses to what's hot and what's not. So please take them only as a guide.

Following the ratings, each chapter lists various details of the cars in the group, with emphasis on the most collectible models. Included are identification tips, historical and technical facts, important specifications, production figures and the strengths and weaknesses of specific cars.

The information in this book is based on my own personal experience as well as my personal contacts' experiences. Hopefully, this material will prove helpful to buyers of vintage Chevrolets.

Investment ratings

Most collector car investments are a function of supply versus demand. Rare models with the most buyers after them generally bring the highest levels of price appreciation in the open market. Such cars usually represent the best investments.

Using original production as a guide, the relative supply of a given car model can be estimated. Some researchers have made "scientific" studies of scrappage rates and/or state registration records to estimate survival of automobiles over specific periods of time from new. Whether the investor uses a rough estimate or the scientific approach, it is still possible to consider the supply factor somewhat objectively in statistical terms.

The demand for a given model is a more subjective factor. For example, the popular 1957 Chevys are not really rare cars, but the demand is high. Therefore, the number of cars available to each potential buyer is relatively low. Opinions about demand reflected by the charts in this book are based on my contact with thousands of Chevrolet collectors.

Only full stars are used to rate the investment potential of the Chevys in this book. This is based on my personal experience with the *Old Cars Price Guide,* which seems to work well as a pricing guide with five condition categories. Theoretically, we could use an infinite number of categories to cover all the various models and options that Chevrolet offered. However, the more specific the research gets, the more subjective the ratings get. It is my feeling that five classifications is a good number to use for an objective approach to gauging the investment market.

Please do not confuse investment potential ratings with a price guide, however. The stars indicate a car's potential to increase in value; they do not relate directly to price. For instance, you might purchase a new Chevy for $14,000 today that would be worth $9,000 in three years. At the same time, an older car costing $1,000 now could be valued at $5,000 in three years. Thus, the older car is a better investment, even though the newer car is more valuable.

Due to the large number of Chevrolet models and options, it has been necessary to consider *only* collectible models in this guide. Mundane cars that rarely or never show up at shows and auctions have been ignored, except for general discussion of appearance and equipment features. Therefore, all cars appearing on the investment rating charts are collectible to one degree or another. This means that even the one-star ratings are for collectible models, rather than ordinary cars, which are not being rated here.

If you happen to be the owner of a car with a one-star rating, remember that this rating is relative to some of the rarest models or model options that Chevrolet made. So, don't put your car up for sale tomorrow. You can still get a lot of enjoyment from it, have lots of fun and watch its value climb as the years go by. It is not likely to skyrocket in value, though. Of course, this may be a benefit; not all of us want to see our hobby cars become unaffordable. The "blue chips" might have great appeal to the speculators, but a lot of us do just fine with our portfolios of "common stocks."

Having written three buyer's guides now, my final advice is still to refer to multiple sources when trying to pinpoint the value and investment potential that your favorite car offers. There are plenty of books available about the collector car market, plus plenty of professional collector car dealers who offer investment advice. Get a few different opinions before making any buying decisions or laying out your hard-earned cash for an antique, special-interest or high-performance automobile.

Star code	Rating	Supply	Demand
★★★★★	Excellent	Very limited	Highest
★★★★	Very good	Below average	High
★★★	Good	Average	Above average
★★	Fair	Above average	Average
★	Poor	High	Low

Chapter 1

1946-48 Stylemaster, Fleetmaster and Fleetline

★★★	1946-48 Fleetmaster convertible
★★★	1946-48 Fleetmaster station wagon
★★	1946-48 Fleetline Aero sedan
★★	1946-48 Fleetmaster coupe and sedan
★★	1946-48 Fleetline Townmaster Sport Sedan
★	1946-48 Fleetmaster Sport Coupe and Sedan
★	1946-48 Stylemaster

Note: Add two stars for Country Club trim kit.

A continuation of 1942 Chevrolets, the 1946-48 models were similar, except for minor trim differences. They came in Stylemaster, Deluxe Fleetmaster and Super Deluxe Fleetline car lines. The last was a fancy Fleetmaster sub-series.

All of these cars had their serial number stamped on a plate on the right windshield post. Chevy also had its own model number system for identification. This was a four-symbol code starting with number 15 for Stylemaster or 21 for Fleetmaster and Fleetline; the last two digits were different for each model. Like other GM divisions, Chevrolet also stamped Fisher body style numbers on the firewall data plate.

Chevrolet six-cylinder engine numbers were stamped on the block near the fuel pump. These numbers are listed in the *Serial Number Book for U.S. Cars 1900-1975.*

Model year can be identified according to grille designs. The 1946 grille had a full outer surround and four veed horizontal bars. In 1947, there was a thick upper bar with the word Chevrolet stamped in it, plus three lower veed horizontal bars. A T-shaped vertical center piece was added to basically the same grille for 1948.

The cars are old-fashioned, but look handsome. Even standard Stylemasters look nice dressed up with two-tone paint and accessories. The only exceptionally rare model is the 1946 station wagon. However, these do not bring more than 1947-48 wagons in the open market, even though a Chevy expert may pay higher for a '46.

Basic specifications were the same for all 1946-48 Chevrolets, regardless of series.

The Chevy overhead-valve six was an inline engine with four-way oiling system combining pressure stream to connecting rods and positive feed to the crankshaft, camshaft and rocker arms. A thermostatic-controlled single downdraft carburetor was used. The engine had full-length water jackets, vacuum advance spark control, a counterbalanced crankshaft, rubber-floated harmonic balancer, lightweight cast alloy iron pistons, and was mounted in a rubber-

The 1946 Chevy Fleetline Aero sedan was part of the high-trim-level series identified by trim bars on fenders. Beltline molding extended onto the hood this year only.

cushioned three-point suspension with two rubber torque-reaction dampers. A 1948 improvement was the introduction of precision interchangeable main bearings.

Ownership

Known for reliability and ease of service, the Chevy six would run a long time with routine service, although it often developed distinct valvetrain noises with abuse. The powerplant did have a history of developing oil leaks at the rear main seal at 50,000 to 60,000 miles. This was considered a typical repair at the time and could sometimes be accomplished using a special tool that reduced the amount of disassembly required. It may be a costly repair today, however. In addition, the fix didn't always take, and a poor mechanic could even make the oil leak worse.

All 1946-48 Chevrolets used a three-speed Synchromesh transmission with helical gears. Its main weakness was cluster gear wear. The clutch was of diaphragm-spring design, with a permanently lubricated ball throw-out bearing. A vacuum power gearshift mechanism was provided for extra-easy movement through the speed ranges. This feature worked great when the cars were new, but sometimes caused trouble later.

A box-girder frame chassis had Chevrolet's Unitized Knee-Action front suspension with ride stabilization and a hypoid drive rear axle (semifloating) with a 4.11:1 standard ratio. Leaf springs were used in the rear. The propeller shaft and universal joints were enclosed in a torque tube. The hydraulic brakes had eleven-inch drums and self-aligning contact shoes.

Electricals were six-volt with sealed-beam headlamps, a foot control high beam switch, front parking lamps, and twin tail and stop lamps. Directional signals were optional. (Any hobby car you drive should have directional lamps for safety.) Stylemasters lacked an automatic door switch dome lamp. The battery was a fifteen-plate, 100 amp six-volt model. A heater was optional, although space for installation was provided below the front seat.

Bodies featured No-Draft ventilation. Door hinges were concealed as were the runningboard-like entrance steps between doors and sills.

Fleetmasters and Fleetlines had bright-metal window frames with decorative bright bars on Fleetline fenders. Pile fabric upholstery was standard in Stylemaster and Fleetmaster bodies; two-tone Bedford cloth was optional in Fleetmasters. Fleetlines used pinstriped mohair upholstery in 1946. In 1947, non-pile Fleetweave fabric was listed in the sales catalog. This was a tan, striped

Fleetmasters for 1946-48 had an upper beltline molding and rocker panel trim, but fenders were plain. The 1946 grille design is seen on this notchback coupe.

The 1947 Fleetmaster club coupe had black rubber gravel guards and gas filler on right-hand rear fender. A small nameplate was now used on the rear sides of the hood. The 1947 grille looked like the 1948 grille without a vertical center bar.

fabric. The 1948 Fleetline featured similar high-quality tan, striped broadcloth seats. Leatherette scuff coverings for front doors and seats were used on both seats in Fleetmaster and Fleetline models, which also had two leather-topped front seat armrests. The front seat, to fit three people, was an adjustable bench with a divided back in two-door models. Each front door and the trunk lid had key locks.

The 1946-48 station wagons were upholstered in tan imitation leather. In 1947, convertibles featured genuine leather seat trim in two tans, two blues and two reds. The 1948 ragtops came with one of each color, except tan, which was replaced with green.

The Chevy six was promoted as a Thriftmaster engine, although its fuel economy was only average. However, gas was cheap and the Chevy powerplant was a good compromise between economy, performance and reliability.

With old age, these 1946-48 Chevys often exhibit body panel fit problems, and original paint may thin or lift in spots. The large pontoon fenders typically show lumps, dings or dents picked up in parking lots or scrapes against garage walls. Interiors usually show some wear and tear, particularly in the seat cushions, with padding sticking out of them. The Fleetmaster and Fleetline models' imitation woodgraining—on door frames especially—is prone to wear. White plastic control knobs and steering wheel rims frequently develop crazing or cracks.

Station wagons were constructed by Cantrell Body Company or Ionia Body Corporation, and consisted of ash framing and mahogany panels. The roof was made of weatherproof grained leatherette stretched over wood slats that show on the inside. Rear windows, in the woodies, slid open or closed and locked by pins. The rear had a liftgate secured by lockable guide brackets, while the tailgate dropped and had two covered chains to support it parallel to the ground. The tailgate interior had wood paneling with brightmetal skid strips. Taillamps were hinged so they would pivot parallel with the ground and shine toward the rear, alerting oncoming traffic of a stopped vehicle or allowing a wagon to be

operated with the gate down. A two-piece rear bumper was used on wagons; a spare tire was mounted on the outside rear in a metal cover.

Prospects

For inexpensive participation in the old-car hobby, you can't beat a good 1946-48 Chevrolet coupe or sedan. They make perfect runaround cars, that is if the engine is tightly sealed, quiet and not blowing excessive blue smoke. Look for cars in fair to excellent shape that don't need much work. An engine overhaul, paint or interior kit can run more money than it costs to buy a good closed car.

Both convertibles and station wagons represent decent investments today, even when minor restoration work is needed, although convertibles sell for slightly more than station wagons. You cannot properly repair a rusty, tattered convertible or a wagon with bad wood inexpensively. That's why their prices are up in the five figures.

The Country Club option was a wood trim kit for the Fleetline Aero sedan and Fleet-

This 1948 Chevy Fleetmaster Sport Coupe has accessories including grille guard, fog lamps, spotlight, window shades and whitewalls. A vertical center member was added to the grille. *Chris Wolfe*

11

In 1948 the Fleetline sub-series continued with stainless steel fender bars. This is the fastback Aero sedan. Whitewalls were in limited supply after the war; black tires were more common.

master coupes and convertible. It was manufactured by Engineered Enterprises of Detroit, and merchandised through selected Chevrolet dealers. Originally priced at $149.50, the option is much more valuable today, since less than ten cars so-equipped are known to exist. Convertibles with this semiaftermarket option represent the top investment you could make in a 1946-48 Chevrolet.

Specifications
1946-48 Chevrolet

Engine	ohv six
Displacement (ci)	216.5
Horsepower (bhp)	90
Wheelbase (in.)	116
Overall length (in.)	197¾
Tires (in.)	6.00×16

A Sport Sedan was also offered in the Fleetline sub-series and was called a Sportmaster sedan. This car, owned by Larry Pester of Saukville, Wisconsin, has optional windshield sun visor, wheel trim rings and white sidewall tires.

Production

Fisher style no.	Chevy model no.	Type vehicle	Production
1946 Stylemaster DJ			
46-1227B	1504	2d Bus Cpe	14,267
46-1227	1524	2d Spt Cpe	19,243
46-1211	1502	2d Twn Sed	61,104
46-1219	1503	4d Spt Sed	75,349
1946 Fleetmaster DK			
46-1027	2124	2d Spt Cpe	27,036
46-1067	2134	2d Conv	4,508
46-1011	2102	2d Twn Sed	56,538
46-1019	2103	4d Spt Sed	73,746
46-Sta Wag	2109	4d Sta Wag	804
1946 Fleetline DK			
46-1069	2113	4d Spt Mas Sed	7,501
46-1007	2144	2d Aero Sed	57,932

Fisher style no.	Chevy model no.	Type vehicle	Production
1947 Stylemaster EJ			
47-1227B	1504	2d Bus Cpe	27,403
47-1227	1524	2d Spt Cpe	34,513
47-1211	1502	2d Twn Sed	88,534
47-1219	1503	4d Spt Sed	42,571
1947 Fleetmaster EK			
47-1027	2124	2d Spt Cpe	59,661
47-1067	2134	2d Conv	28,443
47-1011	2102	2d Twn Sed	80,128
47-1019	2103	4d Spt Sed	91,440
47-Sta Wag	2109	4d Sta Wag	4,912
1947 Fleetline EK			
47-1069	2113	4d Spt Mas Sed	54,531
47-1007	2144	2d Aero Sed	159,407

Fisher style no.	Chevy model no.	Type vehicle	Production
1948 Stylemaster FJ			
48-1227B	1504	2d Bus Cpe	18,396
48-1227	1524	2d Spt Cpe	34,513
48-1211	1502	2d Twn Sed	70,228
48-1219	1503	4d Spt Sed	48,456
1948 Fleetmaster FK			
48-1027	2124	2d Spt Cpe	58,786
48-1067	2134	2d Conv	20,471
48-1011	2102	2d Twn Sed	66,208
48-1019	2103	4d Spt Sed	93,142
48-Sta Wag	2109	4d Sta Wag	10,171
1948 Fleetline FK			
48-1069	2113	4d Spt Mas Sed	83,760
48-1007	2144	2d Aero Sed	211,861

Chapter 2

1949-52 Styleline, Bel Air and Fleetline

★★★	1949-52 Styleline Deluxe convertible
★★★	1949 Styleline Deluxe Ionia station wagon
★★	1950-52 Bel Air two-door hardtop
★★	1949½-52 Styleline Deluxe Fisher station wagon
★	1949-52 Fleetline Deluxe two-door sedan
★	1949-52 Styleline Deluxe Sport and business coupes

Between 1949 and 1952, Chevrolet adopted postwar styling, introduced a hardtop and all-steel station wagon, and brought out its own automatic transmission. Hydraulic valve lifters were introduced, fastbacks lost popularity and Chevy remained America's best-selling car.

The new Chevys had shorter wheelbases. The sedan's height was cut 2½ in. Front thread was 57 in. in 1949-50, 56¹¹⁄₁₆ in. in 1951-52, versus 57⅝ in. in 1948. A 58¾ in. rear tread was used all four years, down from sixty inches. The amount of body glass was up thirty percent. Styling was clean and

All-new Chevy body for 1949 included a grille with curved upper molding and vertical bars below center bar. This Deluxe version has a few bolt-on aftermarket accessories.

Styleline Deluxe Sport Coupe was the name given the fancy two-door sedan in 1949. Deluxe nameplate can be seen near the rear edge of the front fender. Fender skirts were standard for this series.

Again in 1950, notchback models were called Stylelines. Deluxe versions had chrome fender and door moldings, bright gravel guards and skirts. This is the Town Sedan.

rounded, with straight-through front fenders, slab sides and integral inner rear fenders that served as wheelhousings.

Series designations were changed to Special and Deluxe; the Special was the standard trim. Each series had two car lines from 1949-51: Stylelines were notchbacks, Fleetlines were fastbacks.

The 1949-52 Chevrolets had identification numbers and codes similar to the previous models.

Similar grilles were used in 1949 and 1950, but the lower section of the 1949 grille has more (seven) uprights. The hood emblem veed downward in 1949 and slightly upward in 1950. In 1951-52, the grilles again were similar, with a loop of chrome around the lower section. The 1951 upper bar has the Chevrolet name stamped in it. The 1952 upper bar is plain and the center bar has five uprights.

Styleline Specials lack chrome belt moldings and have black rubber gravel shields. Styleline Deluxes have bright belt moldings and chrome gravel shields. Fleetlines are fastbacks, also with bright trim on Deluxes. The word Deluxe appears on the fenders of the more expensive Chevys.

Two types of wagons were sold in 1949. Early in the year, an Ionia-built car with genuine wood was available. At midyear, it was replaced by an all-steel Fisher-built wagon with simulated wood trim.

The 216.5 ci six with solid lifters was used in 1949. Its four main bearings were again of precision interchangeable design. Bore and stroke was 3.5x3.75 in. and the compression ratio was 6.5:1. It developed 90 hp at 3300 rpm and 174 lb-ft of torque at 1600 rpm. A Carter 684S downdraft carburetor was employed.

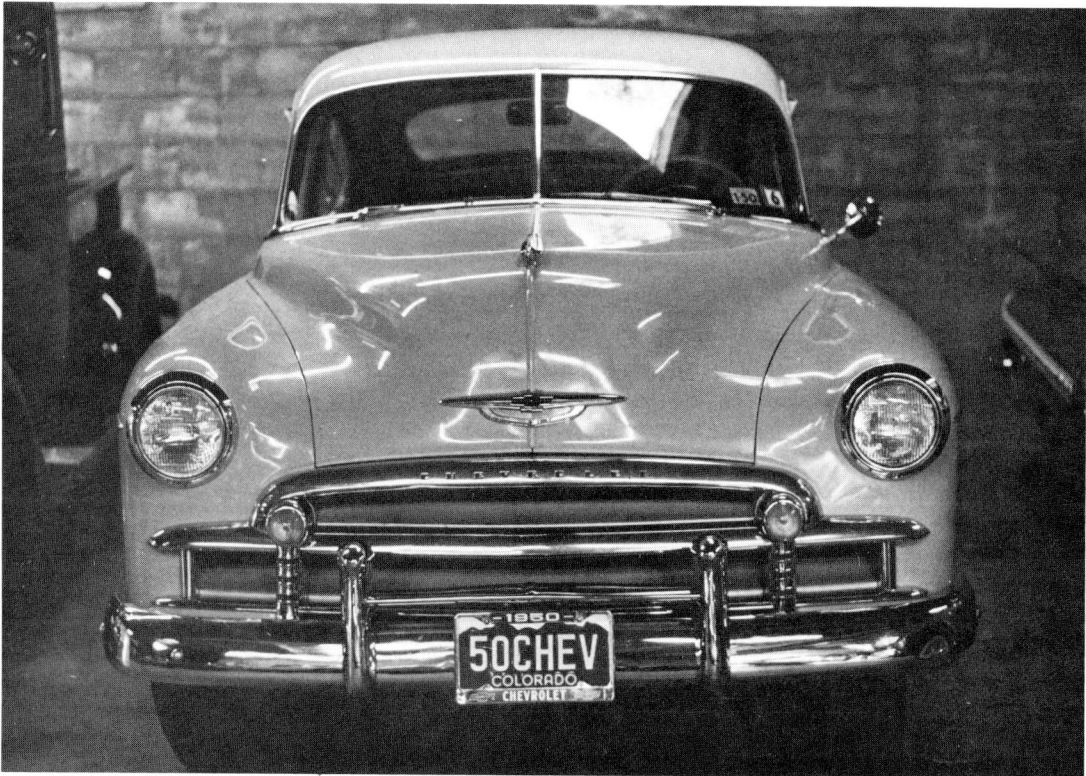

Chevy grille was cleaned up for 1950, with fewer vertical bars in lower section. Grille guard on

Barney Smith's Fleetline Deluxe was a factory accessory. *Chris Wolfe*

Charles Zahnow brought this 1951 Chevy Styleline Deluxe two-door sedan to a car show. Front bodyside molding was positioned lower, but branched over wheel opening at front. Accessories include sun visor, radio and antenna, rear bumper wings and whitewalls.

The base engine for 1950-52 was the same with compression raised to 6.6:1, giving 92 hp at 3400 rpm and 176 lb-ft of torque at 1500 rpm. For 1950-51, Chevy switched to a Rochester Model B downdraft carburetor in all Specials and Deluxes with synchromesh.

With the introduction of automatic transmission (optional in Deluxes only) Chevy used a new 235.5 ci passenger car engine with the new Powerglide drivetrain. It had a 3.56x3.93 inch bore and stroke, and 6.7:1 compression. The lubrication system was the same, except oil under pressure was directed to the self-adjusting hydraulic lifters. Also, the Powerglide engine's cooling system capacity was sixteen quarts instead of fifteen and had a pressurized radiator cap. Transmission oil was water-cooled. Unlike the stick-shift engine's cooling system, the new one did not provide nozzle jet valve seat cooling. It produced 105 hp at 3600 rpm and 198 lb-ft of torque at 1650 rpm.

Jager's 1951 Styleline Deluxe coupe has a longer rear deck and smaller backlight than Zahnow's two-door sedan. Grille guard, back-up lights and exhaust deflector were options.

17

Both 1950 engines had ½ in. diameter exhaust seat valves that were 1/16 in. longer than in 1949. The face angle was changed from thirty to forty-five degrees. Additional metal on the heads and seats, due to this change, increased valve durability. Intake valves on the 235.5 ci engine only, were also larger than in the past (when it was used in trucks). There were accompanying exhaust manifold revisions.

The 1952 engine mounting system was improved by using two supports in front and one at the rear of the transmission. The front mountings were high on each side, instead of low on the extreme front. This eliminated the torque-reaction dampers.

The 1952 216.5 ci engine used a Rochester Model B carburetor with revised idle and accelerating pump circuits (first used with the 1951 Powerglide). A Rochester BC carburetor with automatic choke was used on 1952 Powerglide engines. This carburetor had other refinements.

The two-speed Powerglide was fully automatic, using a hydraulic torque converter with planet gears for reverse and emergency low. The column-mounted manual selector allowed hydraulic control of the transmission and mechanical parking lock control. A safety switch was incorporated into the starter circuit. Maximum torque converter ratio was 2.2:1. A rear axle ratio of 3.55:1 was used with Powerglide.

Chevy's handling and ride quality were improved. The Center-Point seating layout cradled passengers between the wheels. Refinements were made to the Knee-Action with lower control arm improvements from late-1949, on. The center of gravity was lowered by the sleeker new bodies and use of 15 in. tires. And finally, Powerglide cars had heavy-duty front coil springs.

The 1951 grille had no vertical bars; hood emblem had heavier wings. A windshield sun visor was optional. When used, a prismatic traffic-light viewer was installed on top of dash.

The 1951 models had new Jumbo-Drum brakes with Dubl-Life rivetless linings (fifteen percent larger in front) said to require twenty-five percent less pedal pressure. Chevy promoted them as "the largest brakes in the low-priced field." Other innovations were improved Center-Point steering and a new Safety-Sight instrument panel with soft green illumination. The steering gear was of the roll-and-sector type with 17.4:1 ratio on 1949 and early 1950 cars. A 19.4:1 ratio was phased-in during 1950 and used through 1953. New for 1952 were Quick-Reflex sealed-type shock absorbers and an improved Power-Jet carburetion system.

Sedans, coupes and wagons had a box-girder frame. Bel Airs used a similar frame with $5/16$ in. thick triple section siderail reinforcements. To provide additional integrity in convertible bodies, a VK structure of I-beam sections replaced the regular crossmembers.

Two different top motor and pump assemblies (Dura and Moraine) were used in 1949-50 convertibles. They required periodic checks of pump fluid level. Starting in 1951, Chevy provided a "sealed-in" Hydro-Lectric system to operate convertible tops. The new pump was not vented and periodic fluid replacement wasn't required. The top was operated by a self-centering control switch mounted at the bottom of the instrument panel.

Standard equipment in Specials included dual wipers and horns; crease and sill moldings; key-lock doors; black rubber gravel shields; safety glass; rearview mirror; one visor; locking glove compartment; dome light; coat hooks; two-tone gray interiors with striped pattern cloth upholstery; trunk light; and bumper jack with lug wrench.

Deluxes also had brightmetal window moldings; fender moldings; brightmetal gravel shields; fender skirts; twin visors; cigar lighter; ashtray; glovebox light; wind-up clock; two-tone instrument panel; automatic dome lamp switches; armrests; and interior upgrades.

The Bel Air hardtop was introduced in the 1950 Styleline Deluxe series. It was essentially a convertible with a fixed steel roof that swept rearward in an unbroken curve, joining a three-piece wraparound back window. Exclusive monochromatic and two-tone color schemes and interior trims were used.

The 1950 Bel Air's upholstery was gray pile cord with red, green or blue leather trim. Chrome roof bows highlighted the headliner. Courtesy lamps were placed just above the rear inside beltline. Convertibles and Bel Airs had black finish on the steering wheel rim and outer edges of the spokes in 1950, as well as a black gearshift ball. No outside mirror was provided.

For 1951 Bel Airs, black leather trim was added to the other color choices. There were six colorful trims for the 1952 hardtop's interior: tan leather with brown cloth; red or black leather with gray cloth; blue or green leather with matching cloth; and white leather with coral cloth. Four exterior colors and eleven two-tone combinations were available.

The Styleline Deluxe convertible is the model most preferred by 1951 Chevy collectors. It came only in Deluxe trim.

For 1952, Deluxes featured a script nameplate above new gravel guards, which now had a chrome extension onto rear fenders. Front molding was plain like 1950 style, but mounted low as in 1951. Two-tone color combinations were gaining popularity.

A drive report in *Special Interest Autos,* No. 17, evaluated a 1951 Chevrolet convertible with the Powerglide. The hydraulic lifter engine idled without the tappet noise typical of earlier Chevrolets. Steering, handling and brakes got high ratings. The ride quality was soft, with some understeer, but the car felt tight. Using figures from earlier periodicals, economy and performance figures were: best fuel consumption, 23.8 mpg at 30 mph; and average fuel consumption, 18.4 mpg at 50 mph. (From a 1950 *Consumer Research* bulletin.)

For comparison, a stick-shift 1951 coupe belonging to the same collector was driven. It accelerated more briskly and climbed hills better, even with the smaller six.

The 1949-52 continued to be aimed directly at the American mass market and represented a compromise between the best of all worlds. Chevys needed lots of maintenance, but performed well and lasted long when they got it. They were plain looking, but many dress-up accessories were provided to enhance that image.

Ownership and prospects

Until recently, 1949-52 models were inexpensive. Bel Airs, wagons and ragtops are increasing in value. It's too late to buy low and sell high, but they are still good investments. Other closed models are very affordable and great for hobby fun use.

Check the engine carefully for telltale signs of excessive wear or abuse. Stay away from heavy corrosion and rust around the headlamps, rocker panels and rear dog legs. If all looks and runs good, you'll be getting a reliable, low-budget, great-to-play-with car.

Chevy's 1952 grille had "teeth" pressed into center bar. Larger parking lights lacked vent-like decorations. Gordon Jacobson's Bel Air features fog lamps, bumper wings and grille guard. Originally, whitewall tire availability was low due to the Korean War.

Specifications
1949-52 Chevrolet

Engine	ohv six
Displacement (ci)	216.5 ci Synchro; 235.5 ci PG
Horsepower (hp)	90 in 1949; 92 in 1950-52
Wheelbase (in.)	115
Overall length (in.)	197 in 1949, 197½ in 1950, 197^{13}/$_{16}$ in 1951 and 197⅝ in 1952
Tires (in.)	6.70×15 in.

All Deluxes had twin-spoke steering wheels in 1952, plus horn blow ring and ivory control knobs with chrome inserts. Steering wheels for Bel Airs, like Gordon Jacobson's, were extra fancy. Hardtop also had leather and cloth upholstery.

Bel Air hardtops used three-piece rear window; guard to protect trunk was extra, as were bumper end caps. Fender skirts were standard on all Deluxe models, including Bel Air. Blue-Dot taillights are a popular aftermarket accessory.

21

Performance
1951 Chevrolet

0-30 mph	6.02 sec.
0-40 mph	9.55 sec.
0-50 mph	13.75 sec.
Top speed	87.38 mph
0-60 mph	19.35 sec.
0-70 mph	26.05 sec.
Quarter mile	21.05 sec. at 63 mph

Production

Fisher style no.	Chevy model no.	Type vehicle	Production
1949 Styleline Special GJ			
49-1269	1503	4d Sed	46,334
49-1211	1502	2d Sed	69,398
49-1227	1524	2d Spt Cpe	40,239
46-1227B	1504	2d Bus Cpe	20,337
1949 Fleetline Special GJ			
49-1208	1553	4d Sed	58,514
49-1207	1552	2d Sed	36,317
1949 Styleline Deluxe GK			
49-1069	2103	4d Sed	191,357
49-1011	2102	2d Sed	147,347
49-1027	2124	2d Spt Cpe	78,785
49-1067	2134	2d Conv	32,392
49-1061	2109	4d Ionia Sta Wag	3,342
49-1062	2119	4d Fisher Sta Wag	2,664
1949 Fleetline Deluxe GK			
49-1008	2153	4d Sed	130,323
49-1007	2152	2d Sed	180,251

Fisher style no.	Chevy model no.	Type vehicle	Production
1950 Styleline Special HJ			
50-1269	1503	4d Sed	55,644
50-1211	1502	2d Sed	89,897
50-1227	1524	2d Spt Cpe	28,328
50-1227B	1504	2d Bus Cpe	20,984
1950 Fleetline Special HJ			
50-1208	1553	4d Sed	23,278
50-1207	1552	2d Sed	43,682
1950 Styleline Deluxe HK			
50-1069	2103	4d Sed	316,412
50-1011	2102	2d Sed	248,567
50-1027	2124	2d Spt Cpe	81,536
50-1037	2154	2d Bel Air HT	76,662
50-1067	2134	2d Conv	32,810
50-1062	2119	4d Stl Sta Wag	37,100*

Fisher style no.	Chevy model no.	Type vehicle	Production
1950 Fleetline Deluxe HK			
50-1008	2153	4d Sed	124,287
50-1007	2152	2d Sed	189,509

Estimate from a 1952 auto industry trade journal; the figure given in most historical books appears to be incorrect.

Fisher style no.	Chevy model no.	Type vehicle	Production
1951 Styleline Special JJ			
51-1269	1503	4d Sed	63,718
51-1211	1502	2d Sed	75,566
51-1227	1524	2d Spt Cpe	18,981
51-1227B	1504	2d Bus Cpe	17,020
1951 Fleetline Special JJ			
51-1208	1553	4d Sed	3,364
51-1207	1552	2d Sed	6,441
1951 Styleline Deluxe JK			
51-1069	2103	4d Sed	380,270
51-1011	2102	2d Sed	262,933
51-1027	2124	2d Spt Cpe	64,976
51-1037	2154	2d Bel Air HT	103,356
51-1067	2134	2d Conv	20,172
51-1062	2119	4d Stl Sta Wag	23,586
1951 Fleetline Deluxe JK			
51-1008	2153	4d Sed	57,693
51-1007	2152	2d Sed	131,910

Fisher style no.	Chevy model no.	Type vehicle	Production
1952 Styleline Special KJ			
52-1269	1503	4d Sed	35,460
52-1211	1502	2d Sed	54,781
52-1227	1524	2d Spt Cpe	8,906
52-1227B	1504	2d Bus Cpe	10,359
1952 Styleline Deluxe KK			
52-1069	2103	4d Sed	319,736
52-1011	2102	2d Sed	215,417
52-1027	2124	2d Spt Cpe	36,954
52-1037	2154	2d Bel Air HT	74,634
52-1067	2134	2d Conv	11,975
52-1062	2119	4d Sta Wag	12,756
1952 Fleetline Deluxe KK			
52-1007	2152	2d Sed	37,164

Chapter 3

1953-54 Bel Air, 210 and Del Ray

★★★★	1953-54 Bel Air convertible
★★★	1953 210 convertible
★★★	1953-54 Bel Air Sport Coupe
★★	1953-54 Bel Air Townsman station wagon
★★	1953 210 Sport Coupe
★★	1954 210 Del Ray two-door sedan
★	1953-54 Bel Air two- and four-door sedan
★	1953-54 210 Handyman station wagon
★	1953 210 club coupe

New bodies, improved engines and power equipment options are important to 1953-54 Chevrolet buyers. Despite outward similarities, cars of these years have many engineering and product line distinctions.

Bel Airs came in varied body styles and constituted a third, top-level car line, the 2400 series. Next came the Deluxe 210 (2100) series. At the bottom was the Special 150 (1500) series. Certain models were offered only for one year, making them rarer.

Numerical designations with A (Special), B (Deluxe) or C (Bel Air) suffixes replaced two-letter series codes. Otherwise, the veh-

icle identification numbering followed the previous system with codes in the same places as in 1952.

A wider grille with almost twice as many (five) teeth was used in 1954, when parking lamps were changed from round to rectangular shape. Vertical taillamps were seen on both 1952 and 1953 models, but had visored housings in 1954.

Black rubber window gaskets and gravel shields were seen on the 150 models. The 210s had brightmetal trim and simple bodyside moldings. Bel Airs had a double molding treatment on their rear flanks and fender skirts.

The less expensive cars had plain cloth upholstery, while 210s had two-tone fabrics. Seats on Bel Airs had rich, two-tone fabric combinations, complemented by front and rear carpeting. Wagons had vinyl upholstery, while convertibles featured rolled and pleated vinyl. Waffle-patterned vinyl was seen in the 210 club coupe and the late-1954 Del Ray coupe. Bel Air Townsman wagons had simulated woodgrain exterior trim.

Base model specifications were similar, but not exactly the same both years.

There were two engines for both years, the base powerplant for stick-shift cars and a second for Powerglide cars. All had 3.56x 3.81 in. bore and stroke and 235.5 ci. Powerglide cars had slightly higher gross horse-

Base 150 had no side moldings while 1953 210s, like this two-door sedan, had plain full-length chrome strips. Rocker panel molding and rear gravel shield were standard, but chrome shield behind front wheel opening was an accessory.

The 1953 grille had three teeth and large, round parking lamp housings on either side. Vertical guards and protective bumper rail on Jim

Yesse's Bel Air cost extra. The hood ornament shaped like a stylized bird was an extra, too.

power ratings: 115 at 3600 rpm in 1953 and 125 hp at 4000 rpm in 1954. The base 1953 engine's compression ratio was 7.1:1, while all the others had 7.5:1 compression.

Both 1953 engines had cylinder head and valvetrain revisions. A major advance was full-pressure lubrication for the Powerglide cars, which also adopted aluminum pistons, larger valve ports and cooling passages, a new valve cover and shorter, more rigid cylinder head bolts. All Chevys had the Rochester BC single-throat carburetor and automatic choke.

Full-pressure lubrication and aluminum pistons were extended to both engines in 1954. Insert-type rod bearings and more rigid crankshaft and connecting rod bearings were also new. The base Blue Flame 115 powerplant had a revised carburetor power jet valve and higher-pressure radiator cap.

Bel Air no longer meant hardtop; the 1953 series included this four-door sedan. Top car line had double rear moldings with contrasting color insert. Fender skirts were standard on Bel Airs. Massive bumper end caps cost extra, as did whitewalls.

Powerglide engines were quieter because of the new valve cover and use of offset piston pins. Increased combustion efficiency and hydraulic valve lifter life were benefits of a new high-lift camshaft design in Powerglide cars. A cast-iron alloy crankshaft replaced the old forged type in mid-1954, and a cast-iron distributor gear was introduced at the same time. The Powerglide engine also had redesigned alloy iron valve lifters, new XCR steel exhaust valves and a revamped automatic choke that resisted premature opening.

There were several mid-1953 changes to the synchromesh transmission that were carried over into 1954. A new clutch design used spring steel straps for the pressure plate.

The 1953 Powerglide required lifting the control lever slightly to shift from drive to low. A new low-drive valve body design made drive the automatic range in which the vehicle started in low and upshifted automatically. Fluid capacity was also increased and the clutch piston diameter was reduced ½ inch for smoother shifts. The steel drive plates were now of waved design, with new paper-and-cork drive plate facings. Power-

glide refinements for 1954 included improved stator rear thrust washers and a further redesign of the low-drive valve body.

Power steering became optional in 1953. It used a hydraulic power mechanism to assist application of the recirculating ball-type steering gear. Bel Airs and 210s offered power windows and seats in 1954. The new-for-1954 power brakes used engine vacuum to reduce pedal travel fifty percent. Chevrolets with power equipment options, of both years, are relatively rare and most are Bel Airs.

Chevy was obviously after the big car image in 1953-54 styling, particularly for the Bel Air. Both new grilles gave a wider appearance than the year before. Fenderlines, front and rear, were higher and gave the cars a more massive character. In actuality, the bodies were lower and shorter, although they had increased legroom and headroom. One-piece, curved wraparound glass was used for windshields and rear windows. Paint colors and two-tone combinations were much brighter.

Standard in 150s was a plain horn button steering wheel, one sun visor, two windshield wipers and rubber floor mats. The 210s also had foam rubber seat cushions, full-circle steering wheel horn rings, two

Ribbed trim plates were used on front body corners of 1953 Chevys. The Chevy emblem on front of hood was redesigned. Full wheel covers shown here were a feature of Bel Airs. Jim McCarthy, of Burlington, Wisconsin, owns this car.

Distinctive taillight lens was used on all 1953 Chevys. The Bel Airs' roof pillars had a decorative plate. No-Mar fuel guard door kept gas station attendants from scratching paint.

sun visors, brightmetal control knob inserts and rear compartment carpeting. Bel Airs added a Deluxe horn button, extra-wide chrome window reveals on sedans, windshield pillar cover and saddle moldings on hardtops and convertibles, brightmetal roof bows in hardtops and full carpeting. Powerglide was optional for 210s and Bel Airs in 1953. All Chevy buyers could order it in 1954.

Buyers found the most extensive model line-up ever in 1953—sixteen different cars. This was reduced to fourteen in 1954 though, when the 210 convertible, Sport Coupe and eight-passenger wagon disappeared. An eight-passenger Bel Air wagon was added, however, and the 150 business coupe became the Utility sedan, a coupe with a raised loadspace (instead of seat) in the rear compartment.

There were thirteen solid paint colors and eleven two-tones in 1953, plus twenty-nine interior trims. For 1954, there were fourteen solids, thirteen two-tones and thirty interior options. Codes indicating original paint and trims can be found on a Chevrolet's firewall data plate.

Motor Trend reviewed a 210 sedan with Powerglide in 1954. Many minor criticisms— insufficient forward vision, right rear door blind spot, transmission hum at idle, road noise, rear brake lockup and a "floundering" ride quality—were similar to problems found in the 1953 Chevrolet road test.

The magazine liked the neatly laid out, fully instrumented dash and "screen door-like" spare tire holddown. Steering (manual) was described as "the usual easy Chevrolet setup with many turns." Engine accessibility was praised, but steering wheel vibrations were scored low.

A lower top speed (94.2 mph) was noted for the 1954 car, compared to the 1953 Powerglide. However, its fuel consumption was 15.1 mpg for 632 miles, nearly two miles per gallon less than the '53.

The 210 went from 0-60 mph in 18.9 seconds and did the quarter-mile in 19.9 at 66 mph. Stopping distances were forty-three feet at 30 mph, eighty-nine feet at 45

The 1954 Chevy grille had five teeth on a wider horizontal center bar; parking lamps were housed in wraparound grille extensions. This base 150 model has no side trim.

mph and 149 feet at 60 mph, which was good for the era. *Motor Trend* estimated the cost of operating a Chevy at 2.6 cents per mile and the cost of ownership (including financing) at 8.4 cents per mile. The 210 was summed up as "a car that won't set the connoisseurs aflame with desire, but will serve a colossal number of new-car buyers in a way thoroughly calculated to please them year in and year out."

Ownership and prospects

Collectors may find the 1953-54 Chevys pleasing, too. They've never set the investment market aflame, either, although Bel Air convertibles and Sport Coupes are starting to climb in price. Serious fans may be hot for a 1953 210 ragtop or hardtop, because of low production. However, the Bel Airs are really the blue chips. Wagons are interesting, but not really stylish or rare, except for the 1954 Townsman. This particular eight-passenger is worth a second look.

The first thing to look for, as a buyer, is the condition of front end trim. With Korean War material restrictions, inferior plating that rarely holds up well was used on the 1953 grille. To make matters worse, some poorly plated parts are made of pot metal; when the chrome goes, they pit up badly. Replacement grilles are hard to find, but if they're solid metal, they can be replated. Better quality plating brightened the 1954 grilles, but the parking lamp housings are notorious for rust-through. Reproductions are available, but expensive.

As in earlier years, poorly maintained Stovebolt sixes are common (and noisy). Chevys required oil changes every 2,000-3,000 miles, lubes every 1,000 miles and tune-up, tire and brake service at 5,000 mile intervals. Many owners skimped on maintenance and their cars suffered. When inspecting a prospect for purchase, check carefully for excessive lifter clatter, blue exhaust smoke and oil leaks at the rear main seal.

Convertible was offered only as a Bel Air for 1954, since the 210 ragtop was dropped in mid-1953. Heavy chrome windshield frame was featured on the open model. *Chris Wolfe*

Figure into the price a minimum of $1,000 for a decent overhaul. Transmission hum, you'll recall, was normal.

These cars will usually start to rust in the floorboards or front fender corners. If not checked, corrosion will extend to rocker panels and below the rear window. However, the driver's floorboard is the place to start checking. Rust isn't a frequent problem, however; trim deterioration is much more common.

Overall, the 1953-54 Chevys are good cars to play around with for some hobby fun. They're basically reliable, easy-to-drive vehicles that look attractive when colorfully painted, especially with Bel Air trim. But,

except for convertibles, don't expect anything crazy like huge price leaps. The investment picture is only a modest one.

Specifications
1953-54 Chevrolet

Engine	ohv six
Displacement (ci)	235.5
Horsepower (bhp)	108 in 1953; 115 in 1954
Wheelbase (in.)	115
Overall length (in.)	195.5 in 1953; 196.5 in 1954
Tires (in.)	6.70×15

In addition to a two-door hardtop (called a Sport Coupe), the 1954 Bel air also came as the two-door sedan shown here. Chevy adopted the one-piece windshield in 1953. *Chris Wolfe*

29

Production

Fisher style no.	Chevy model no.	Type vehicle	Production
1953 Special 1500A (150)			
53-1269	1503	4d Sed	54,207
53-1211	1502	2d Sed	79,416
53-1227	1524	2d Clb Cpe	6,993
53-1227B	1504	2d Bus Cpe	13,555
53-1262F	1509	2d Sta Wag	22,408
1953 Deluxe 2100B (210)			
53-1069W	2103	4d Sed	332,497
53-1011W	2102	2d Sed	247,455
53-1027	2124	2d Clb Cpe	23,961
53-1037	2154	2d Spt Cpe	14,045
53-1067	2134	2d Conv	5,617
53-1062F	2109	4d Sta Wag (6P)	18,258
53-1062	2119	4d Sta Wag (8P)	7,988
1953 Super Deluxe Bel Air 2400C			
53-1069WD	2403	4d Sed	246,284
53-1011WD	2402	2d Sed	144,401
53-1037D	2454	2d Spt Cpe	99,047
53-1067D	2434	2d Conv	24,047

Fisher style no.	Chevy model no.	Type vehicle	Production
1954 Special 155A (150)			
54-1269W	1503	4d Sed	32,430
54-1211W	1502	2d Sed	64,855
54-1262F	1509	4d Sta Wag	21,404
54-1211WB	1512	2d Utl Sed	10,770
1954 Deluxe 2400B (210)			
54-1069W	2103	4d Sed	235,146
54-1011W	2102	2d Sed	194,498
54-1011WA	2124	2d Del Ray Cpe	66,403
54-1062	2109	4d Sta Wag	27,175
1954 Bel Air 2400C			
54-1069WD	2403	4d Sed	248,750
54-1011WD	2402	2d Sed	143,573
54-1037	2454	2d Spt Cpe	66,378
54-1067D	2434	2d Conv	19,383
54-1062D	2419	2d Sta Wag	8,156

Chapter 4

1955-57 Bel Air, 210 and 150

★★★★★	1955-57 Bel Air convertible
★★★★	1955-57 Bel Air Sport Coupe and Nomad
★★★	1955-57 Bel Air (all other models)
★★★	1955-57 210 Sport Coupe and Del Ray
★★	1955-57 210 (all other models)
★	1955-57 150 (all models)

Powerful V-8s, twelve-volt electrics, tubeless tires, ball joints, overdrive and lower, modern bodies highlighted the 1955 classic Chevy. Appearance changes for 1956 included a facelift and racier trim. Heftier engines and a four-door hardtop were also introduced. The 1957 had tail fins and more chrome. A new 283 ci V-8 had Corvette per-

Ferrari-inspired egg-crate grille was new for 1955 Chevrolets, along with wedge-shaped front parking lamp housings. Chevy hood emblem was wider and thinner and a new bumper was seen.

Back-up lamp wiring was optional for 1955 Chevys, but all cars had this type of taillamp lens designed for back-ups. Foxcraft fender skirts were a popular aftermarket item, since the factory did not supply them. Lack of V-8 emblem below taillamp indicates this convertible is six-cylinder powered.

formance options including dual four-barrel carburetors or Ramjet fuel injection. There were several new transmissions: Corvette Powerglide, Turboglide or close-ratio three-speed.

Serial numbers began with a V on V-8s. The 1955-56 engine codes had a Z (six) or G (V-8) suffix. Beginning in 1957, coding got more complex.

The 150s, 210s and Bel Airs were offered again. The 1955s had a cellular egg-crate grille. A full-width type with rectangular parking lamps came in 1956. The 1957s had an oval-shaped grille with round bumper "bombs." Specifications for the three years were similar, but not identical.

The 1955 150 had no side moldings. The 210s had a vertical saddle molding joining a rear fender spear. Bel Airs added a front fender/door spear and model nameplates.

In 1956, the 150s had a saddle molding and front fender/door spear. The 210 sweep-spears continued rearward in a downward

Two-toning on Bel Airs was applied in a new manner with upper rear fenders, trunk lid and rear sheet metal in same color as the roof. This is the Bel Air Sport Coupe. *Chris Wolfe*

curve to the back bumper. Bel Airs used a double rear sweepspear and had a front fender nameplate.

The 1957 150 sweepspears compared to 1955 210s', while new trim for the middle car line consisted of full-length curved sweepspears. A second molding on the rear door or fender duplicated the shape of the year's tail fins. On 1957 Bel Airs, the space between the double rear moldings had a silver annodized insert. Triple front fender chevrons, rear fender nameplates and bright rocker panel moldings were seen, too.

The 150s had rubber floor coverings, one inside visor and pattern cloth (vinyl in wagons) upholstery. Model 210s added such items as a second visor, glovebox light, ashtray, cigar lighter, automatic dome lamp switches, horn ring, foam seats and richer fabrics (vinyl in wagons and Del Ray). Bel Airs also had carpeting, a three-spoke steering wheel, electric clock, full wheel discs and dressier two-tone upholstery in gabardine, pattern cloth and vinyl combinations.

Chevy offered fifteen solid and twenty-four two-tone paint schemes in 1955, plus forty-two interior combinations (seven genuine leather trims for the new Nomad, a two-door station wagon with sporty hardtop styling). On two-toned cars, the second color was available on the roof only or on the roof, rear deck and upper rear quarters. For 1956, there were thirteen solid colors, nineteen two-tones and fifty-one interior choices. The 1957 models came in sixteen solid colors and fifteen two-tones and offered forty-eight interior codes. Convertibles featured cloth and imitation leather upholstery.

Many companies manufacture 1955-57 Chevy reproduction interior kits. These firms can provide information and samples of fabrics based on data plate codes.

Wide interior selections reflected Chevy's desire to capture a big-car look, especially for Bel Airs. The 1955 cars were very much patterned after the Cadillac image with eye-browed headlamps, eagle hood ornaments, wraparound windshields and Caddy-like taillamps.

Like bigger cars, Chevys now came with an optional V-8 used in seventy-eight percent of production. This engine was small,

light and cheap to build. It measured thirty-four inches high, 26½ in. wide and 34⁴/₅ in. long, representing a hot-rodder's dream, because it fit into many chassis. The base version was a two-barrel job with 162 hp. Later came a Power-Pack option with four-barrel carburetor, dual exhausts and 180 hp. A special-order 190 hp performance option was issued in June of that year.

The base 123 hp six with solid valve lifters was available in any Chevy. Powerglide sixes

Bel Air's fancier trim included a script-style model nameplate and gold Chevy crest behind "saddle" molding. Dash-like indentations on saddle molding were painted black while rear horizontal sweepspear had a white-painted insert.

Wraparound one-piece windshield appeared in 1955. The 210s had chrome window frames. Two-tones in this series were applied with only the roof in the second color.

had hydraulic lifters and thirteen more horsepower. The Powerglide automatic was also improved. On stick-shift cars, a Warner gear overdrive was optional. This was a first for Chevrolet or any General Motors car.

The small-block Chevy V-8 had three important innovations. New green sand-block casting techniques kept production costs low. A stamped rocker arm was another cost-cutter that also eliminated misalignment and cocking problems common with shaft-mounted rockers. New hollow hydraulic lifter pushrods did a good job lubricating the top end of all engines.

Chevrolet front suspensions were improved by the use of ball joints and by the angling of upper and lower control arms to prevent dive when braking. *Motor Trend* honored 1955-56 models as its "best handling" automobile. *Consumer Reports* gave 1955 handling a special mention. Other new features included ball race steering; suspended pedals; high-level ventilation; push-button door handles; Hotchkiss drive (no more torque tube); and tubeless tires. Air conditioning was offered for 1955 V-8s, except convertibles. Directional signals were still optional.

Motor Trend tested a 210 four-door sedan in its January 1955 issue and praised the 162 hp V-8's exceptional handling and overall design. Headroom and legroom were good, the ride was fairly soft and fit and finish was highly rated. The magazine liked Chevy's new central glove compartment, vision through the wraparound windshield, wiper operation, lack of blind spots, new steering wheel location and positioning of controls and gauges.

According to *Motor Trend,* the car accelerated better than all others, except Cadillac and Buick Century, and was capable of staying with Chryslers, Lincolns and Oldsmobiles. Ride, handling and ease of control also scored high marks, and brakes were rated better than average for the era. Spark plug accessibility and limited seat adjustment were the magazine's only real criticisms.

Model year 1956 brought a new, wider lattice-style grille, flatter and longer hood, revised side trim, more glittery taillights (the left lamp hid the fuel filler) and reshaped wheel openings. Two-tone paint schemes were revised to achieve a lower, wider and longer appearance. There were several important additions to engine offerings, as the horsepower race got in gear.

Featuring the basic styling of a Sport Coupe, the Bel Air Nomad station wagon was introduced in January 1955 at the Waldorf Astoria Hotel in New York. Special Nomad features included front molding with white insert and heavy chrome eyebrows above headlights.

Bel Air script and Chevy crest were the only trim items used on Nomad rear fenders, unless V-8 engines were ordered. This car has the V-8 emblems under the taillights. The Nomad tailgate had seven vertical rub strips to distinguish it.

The 1956 Chevy's hood ornament resembled the "bird" type of 1955 with longer tailfeathers. A grooved parking lamp extension plate decorates body corner. Bud Adams, of Mosinee, Wisconsin, was the owner of this 210 two-door sedan.

Chevy sixes used a new 140 hp hydraulic lifter Blue Flame engine. Then came the carry-over 162 hp (170 hp with Powerglide) Turbo-Fire V-8. The next option was the Super Turbo-Fire V-8 with 9.25:1 compression, a four-barrel, dual exhausts, higher-lift camshaft and special intake manifolds. It was rated for 205 hp. At the top was the 225 hp Corvette V-8 with dual four-barrels, twin air cleaners, a special high-lift cam, high-speed mechanical valve lifters, high-power exhaust headers and dual exhausts.

The Corvette engine was first listed as an "on request" item, because Chevy's 1955 Corvette solid lifter engine had durability and noise problems. *Popular Science* said Chevy engineers advised that hydraulic lifters had been reworked to handle up to 5300 rpm. However, the Corvette engine, with solid lifters, was later made a regular passenger car option. Other minor improvements for the season included the change to

Cars in the Bel Air line had a model namescript and gold Chevy crest on the rear fenderside in 1956. Bodyside molding treatment created new two-toning possibilities. Large taillamp housings were chrome-trimmed with bullet-shaped lens.

a full-flow oil filter, stronger generator mountings and heavy-duty clutches with high-horsepower stick-shift cars.

Special Interest Autos (August 1983) tested the new-for-1956 Bel Air four-door hardtop—or Sport Sedan—with the base 170 hp Powerglide V-8. Although it leaned quite a bit in turns, the car was found to handle well. Steering (nonpower) was somewhat vague and the tires scrubbed a bit during hard cornering. The brakes were adequate, though not well-matched to engine performance. Overall, the enthusiast magazine described the car as adequate: "An average automobile that offered good dollar value, was enjoyable to drive, easy to maintain and economical to operate." Contemporary road-testers complained about limited seat adjustment, the small rearview mirror, weak seat springs and limited rear seat headroom in Sport Sedans.

A "cult car" today, the 1957 Chevy was basically a modified 1956 with extensive outer sheet metal revisions and a completely redesigned shelf-like instrument panel. Everything about the car was brighter and more up to date.

Base engine was again the Blue Flame 140 six. The 265 ci V-8 was available, but only for stick-shift and overdrive cars; this was the two-barrel version with a new 8.5:1 compression ratio. Although Chevrolet ads promoted five engines, there actually were six other options, for a total of eight different horsepower choices.

Two-toning on 1956 Bel Air Sport Coupe featured second color for side spears, rear fenders, deck lid and roof. Full wheel covers were again a standard Bel Air feature.

A brand-new body style for 1956 was the four-door hardtop or Sport Sedan. It was available as a 210 or the Bel Air shown here.

36

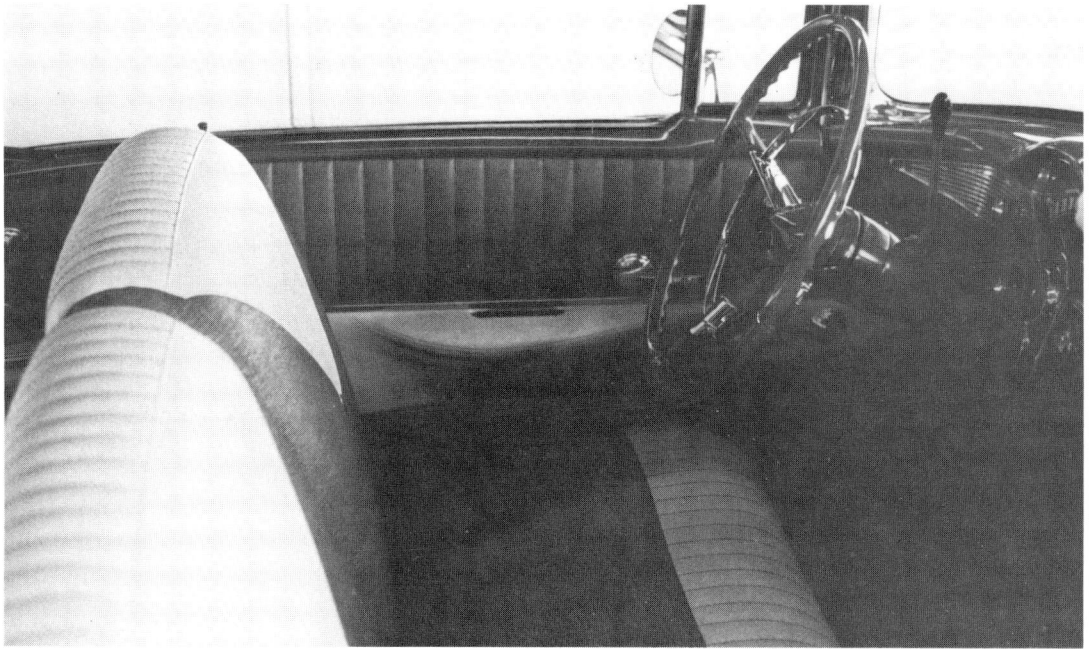

The 1956 convertible's interior featured pattern cloth and imitation leather. All Bel Airs had the three-spoke steering wheel with V-shaped horn button emblem for V-8s.

The Nomad returned in 1956 with body trim more like that of other Bel Airs. As in 1955, the rear side windows were sliders and the rear of the roof had horizontal ribs running fully across it. *Chris Wolfe*

The 1957 210 models had an upgraded trim level with full-length bodyside moldings and a painted insert between the two rear moldings. Optional full wheel covers appear on this 1957 210 wagon owned by Lee Joyce of Madison, Wisconsin.

The 210 station wagons were known as Townsman models. On all 210s, a Chevrolet namescript was placed at the upper edge of the painted insert. One-piece rear side glass was used here.

Both the original 265 ci V-8 and new 283 ci had several new features: fuel filters; larger ports; wide bearings; lubrication improvements; redesigned clutches; a balance tube for dual exhausts; new distributor; and refined electrical system.

Body styling again sought the lower and longer image, and a new ventilation system employed scoops in the upper headlamp bezels for fresh air intake. This eliminated cowl vents and permitted a height reduction. At the rear, the fuel filler was hidden behind a molding on the left-hand tail fin. Taillamps were housed in chrome protuberances that resembled exhaust ports.

The new instrument cluster was called a Flight Panel and had gauges grouped so they could easily be seen through the recessed steering wheel hub (the 1955-56 models had been criticized because the steering wheel blocked instrument panel visibility). The radio speaker was located in the center of the upper shelf, below a grille, to keep the sound from blaring directly at passengers. However, this location made the speakers more susceptible to the effects of sunlight and heat, which promoted early deterioration.

The new two-speed Turboglide automatic transmission was somewhat similar to Buick's Dynaflow. It incorporated three turbines and two planetary gearsets in combination with a variable-pitch stator and conventional torque converter pump. This design provided an infinitely variable torque ratio for smooth acceleration from start to full speed. Turboglide was a complex unit that proved prone to failure and difficult to repair, however. It performed well when new, but did not have the reliability of GM's Hydra-Matic. By 1961, Chevrolet abandoned the Turboglide.

Other changes in 1957 included the switch to fourteen-inch tires and the revision of rear axle ratios. Brake linings and brake springs were improved. Chevrolet also added more braces to its chassis and refined ball joints, shock absorbers and rear leaf springs. However, the new front end was heavier and had a slightly adverse effect on handling.

When nearly new, the early 1955 models drew significant complaints from owners about excessive oil consumption. Chevrolet addressed this in an engineering statement that said the problem was due to slow seating of chrome oil rings. Another problem was that a greater than imagined amount of oil was delivered to the valves. There were also reports—said to be unfounded—that the stamped rocker arms were failing. The biggest problem, though, was with the Corvette engines with solid lifters.

Ownership

At any rate, if you're interested in buying a 1955-57 Chevy, the chances are pretty slim you'll be worrying about problems that were once fairly typical, like rusty front fender eyebrows on 1955-56 models or worn-out engines. Most of the cars in the marketplace have been at least partly restored because their value is high and reproduction parts are easy to get. Since these cars are in such high demand and easy to sell, it pays for owners to fix obvious flaws before bringing them to market.

At the same time, the level of knowledge about the cars is high and this makes authenticity a critical factor. To get top value for your money, it's important to invest in a "classic" Chevy that's "correct" in

The V-shaped insignia on the tailgate of Lee Joyce's station wagon indicates a V-8 model. Tailgate is hinged at bottom; upper liftgate features one-piece window.

terms of matching serial numbers, paint colors, upholstery and optional equipment. That's not to say that condition doesn't count, but it *is* possible to find an original car in good shape that could be worth more than a doctored-up example that appears to be completely restored.

Prospects

The model year, trim level and assortment of options of a classic Chevy are tremendously significant to collectors. In general, the 1957 models are most desirable, followed by the 1955s and 1956s in that order. Bel Air is the preferred trim level, even though some of the less expensive models may be rarer and more unusual. At the top of the investment or pricing picture are convertibles. Sport Coupes come next, then the Nomad two-door wagons with hardtop styling. The choice extras are the hot (in a performance sense) drivetrain options like fuel injection or dual four-barrel carburetors. When they were new, *Motor Trend* said "only a midget's handful of citizens are making payments on fuel injected cars." Today, there may be more 1955-57 Chevys with this option than there were thirty years ago.

If you are a serious collector with tons of money to spend, the Bel Air ragtops, hardtops and Nomads may be of interest. However, keep in mind some of the recent prices. At one auction last year, a pair of near-perfect 1957s—hardtop and convertible— were bid to $90,000 and *not* sold. A few months later, another 1957 ragtop did

Bel Air trim on 1957 Sport Coupe featured bright rocker panel moldings and slashes of chrome on sides of front fender near headlamps. Bumper guards were factory accessory.

Bel Airs featured a ribbed, annodized insert between the double rear fender moldings. It was decorated with a Bel Air script and Chevrolet crest. This four-door sedan is a six-cylinder version, judging from lack of V-shaped insignia on trunk lid.

change hands for $50,000! You need a big bankroll to play in that kind of marketplace.

Even so, these are still the investment cars. In the same period that 1957 convertibles leaped from $25,000 to $50,000, the Nomad wagons went from about $15,000, to $22,000. Just about all of these cars are climbing fast in value, but at widely varying rates.

The Nomads look like a good buy in terms of body style. They are pretty and rare and the Nomad Club has just been revitalized, which may start the prices upward again. There are also some good buys on Bel Air hardtops around.

When it comes to the different vintages, the 1956 models are worth a long look. They still haven't gone wild yet; however, many experts consider them the prettiest of the lot and expect above-average appreciation to hit soon. The 210s are beginning to pick up steam as the supply of Bel Airs dwindles, so the rarer cars in this series, as well as Bel Air sedans and wagons, seem like good mid-range investments.

Generally speaking, as an investment the V-8s are the way to go, no matter what model you're looking at. And the more options on the car, the better your money will be spent. As a pure investment, stay away from modified cars. They have a lot of appeal to younger enthusiasts, but are generally hard to move and difficult to obtain top dollar for in the established collector market.

Specifications
1955-57 Chevrolet

Engine	ohv six
Displacement (ci)	235.5
Horsepower (bhp)	123 in 1955; 140 in 1956-57
Wheelbase (in.)	116
Overall length (in.)	195.6 in 1955; 197.5 in 1956; 202.8 in 1957
Tires (in.)	6.70×15 in 1955-56; 7.50×14 in 1957

A true cult car of 1950s America, the 1957 Chevrolet Bel Air convertible commands high prices in today's collector car market. This one has optional grille guards and a spotlight.

This unusual 1957 Chevy is a factory-built stretch limousine owned by John Boldt of Kaukana, Wisconsin. It has Bel Air trim and an accessory-type beauty panel at the base of the rear deck lid. This panel matches the bodyside inserts on rear fenders, and was available for all Bel Airs.

Continuing to provide a sporty station wagon with two-door hardtop roofline, Chevrolet made the 1957 Bel Air Nomad available in a wider choice of colors. Full wheel covers were standard on all Bel Airs. *Chevrolet Motor Division*

Performance
1955 Chevrolet

	235.5 ci 123 hp six	265.5 ci 162 hp V-8
0-60 mph	12.3 sec.	15.3 sec.
¼ mile	19 sec. at 71 mph	19.9 sec. at 70 mph
Avg top speed	97.3 mph	95.7 mph
Tank avg fuel	14.5 mpg	19.3 mpg

1956 Chevrolet

	265.5 ci 205 hp V-8
0-60 mph	10.7 sec.
¼ mile	18.3 sec. at 76 mph
Avg top speed	108.7 mph
Tank avg fuel	14.2 mpg

1957 Chevrolet

	283 ci 270 hp V-8
0-60 mph	9.9 sec.
¼ mile	17.5 sec. at 77.5 mph
Avg top speed	—
Tank avg fuel	15 mpg

Engines
1957 Chevrolet

Ci	C.R.	Induction	Exhaust	Hp@rpm	Valve lifters
Turbo-Fire V-8					
283	8.5:1	2V	single	185@4600	hydraulic
Super Turbo-Fire V-8					
283	9.5:1	4V	dual	220@4800	hydraulic
Corvette V-8					
283	9.5:1	2×4V	dual	245@5000	hydraulic
283	9.5:1	FI	dual	250@5600	hydraulic
283	9.5:1	2×4V	dual	270@6000	solid
283	10.5:1	FI	dual	283	solid

Production

Fisher style no.	Chevy model no.	Type vehicle	Production
1955 150			
55-1219	1503	4d Sed	29,898
55-1211	1502	2d Sed	66,416
55-1211B	1512	2d Utl Sed	11,196
55-1263F	1529	2d Sta Wag	17,936
1955 210			
55-1019	2103	4d Sed	317,724
55-1011	2102	2d Sed	249,105
55-1011A	2124	2d Clb Cpe	115,584
55-1037F	2154	2d Spt Cpe	11,675
55-1063F	2129	2d Sta Wag	29,918
55-1062F	2109	4d Sta Wag	82,303
1955 Bel Air			
55-1019	2403	4d Sed	345,372
55-1011D	2402	2d Sed	168,313
55-1037D	2454	2d Spt Cpe	185,562
55-1067D	2434	2d Conv	41,292
55-1064DF	2429	2d Nomad Sta Wag	6,103
55-1062DF	2409	4d Sta Wag	24,313

Fisher style no.	Chevy model no.	Type vehicle	Production
1956 150			
56-1219	1503	4d Sed	51,544
56-1211	1502	2d Sed	82,384
56-1211B	1512	2d Utl Sed	9,879
56-1263F	1529	2d Sta Wag	13,487
1956 210			
56-1019	2103	4d Sed	283,125
56-1039	2113	4d Spt Sed	20,021
56-1011	2102	2d Sed	205,545
56-1011A	2124	2d Cpe	56,382
56-1037	2154	2d Spt Cpe	18,616
56-1063F	2129	2d Sta Wag	22,038
56-1062F	2109	4d Sta Wag	113,656
56-1062FC	2119	4d Sta Wag (3S)	17,988
1956 Bel Air			
56-1019D	2403	4d Sed	269,798
56-1039D	2413	4d Spt Sed	103,602
56-1011D	2402	2d Sed	104,849
56-1037D	2454	2d Spt Cpe	128,382
56-1067D	2434	2d Conv	41,268
56-1064DF	2429	2d Nomad	7,886
56-1062DF	2419	4d Beauville	13,268

Note: Production includes 6-cyl and V-8.

Fisher style no.	Chevy model no.	Type vehicle	Production
1957 150			
57-1219	1503	4d Sed	52,266
57-1211	1502	2d Sed	70,774
57-1211B	1512	2d Utl Sed	8,300
57-1263F	1529	2d Sta Wag	14,740
1957 210			
57-1019	2103	4d Sed	260,401
57-1039	2113	4d Spt Sed	16,178
57-1011	2102	2d Sed	162,090
57-1011A	2124	2d Del Ray Cpe	25,664
57-1037	2154	2d Spt Cpe	22,631
57-1062F	2109	4d Sta Wag	27,803
57-1062FC	2119	4d Sta Wag (3S)	21,083
57-1063	2129	2d Sta Wag	17,528
1957 Bel Air			
57-1019D	2403	4d Sed	254,331
57-1039D	2413	4d Spt Sed	137,672
57-1011D	2402	2d Sed	62,751
57-1037D	2454	2d Spt Cpe	166,426
57-1067D	2434	2d Conv	47,562
57-1062DFC	2409	4d Townsman	27,375
57-1064DF	2429	2d Nomad	6,103

Note: Production includes 6-cyl and V-8.

Chapter 5

1958-60 Bel Air and Impala

★★★★   1958 Bel Air Impala
            convertible
★★★   1958 Bel Air Impala
            Sport Coupe
★★★   1959-60 Impala
            convertible
★★   1959-60 Impala Sport Coupe
★★   1958-60 Bel Air Sport
            Coupe and Nomad
★   1958-60 Impala and
            Bel Air Sport Sedan

Chevy's 1958 season featured all-new Sculpturamic gull-wing styling, the first Impalas, full-coil suspensions and a bigger Turbo-Thrust V-8. Buyer interest in the failure-prone Level Air suspension option quickly deflated, however. Chevy marketed its third totally redesigned car in as many years for 1959. It had improved Safety-Master brakes and acrylic paint. Impalas became a separate car line. The compact Corvair was 1960's big news, relegating changes in full-size cars to a facelift.

Serial numbers used an A (six) or B (V-8) as the first symbol on bottom series cars; a C (six) or D (V-8) on mid-price cars; and an E (six) or F (V-8) on top-line models. Next came a 58, 59 or 60 indicating model year, then a plant code: A=Baltimore; F=Flint; J=Janesville; K=Kansas City; L=Los Angeles; N=Norwood; O=Oakland; S=St. Louis; T=Tarrytown; and (in 1959-60) W=Willow Run. The last six numbers indicated production sequence.

Check grilles for quick model-year identification. In 1958, dual headlamps were positioned above an oval grille housing twin-lens parking lamps. For 1959, dual headlamps were mounted alongside the toothy grille, with parking lamps in cat's-eye openings in the fenders above. In 1960, the grille returned to an oval shape. It had a horizontal bar insert with crossbar trim. Parking lamps were placed right in the bumper.

In 1958, the cars were (bottom to top) Del Rays, Biscaynes and Bel Airs. Del Rays had single bodyside moldings that curved slightly downward at the rear. The Biscayne moldings were similar, except there were two on the front with bright window trim. Bel Airs had straight, full-length body moldings (fluted in front) connected to the rear fender contour moldings by short pieces of diagonal chrome. Two Bel Air Impalas added air scoop rear-quarter ornaments, fancier front fender trim and rocker panel moldings. The Impala hardtop had a roof air scoop, and both models had an extra (third) taillamp on each side.

The Biscayne was the low-price line in 1959. A solid molding decorated front fenders, extending to the door. Next came the Bel Air, with front fender crests and full-length side moldings with painted in-

Del Ray series offered the plainest 1958 Chevys. This is the Yeoman two-door, six-passenger station wagon. All wagons had a single taillamp treatment. Del Rays had no bodyside trim.

45

John Larsen's 1958 Chevy Biscayne two-door sedan illustrates the new wide grille, dual headlamps and dual parking lamps adopted that season. Lack of a V-shaped decoration below hood emblem reveals this car is a six. Full wheel covers were a Biscayne option.

John Larsen's 1958 Biscayne has the correct type of chrome exhaust deflector, but the fox tails are a personal touch. The small square below deck lid, on the left, is the fuel filler door.

serts. Top-level Impalas had crossed flag emblems on their painted insert area on the bodyside moldings, front fender crown moldings and other special trim.

The series for 1960 remained unchanged. All Chevys had rocketship rear fender ornaments, with a painted section on Impalas. Bel Airs had window frame moldings and rear panel outline moldings. Impalas had a trimmed beauty panel at the rear and three (instead of two) taillamp housings on each side, plus chrome front fender slashes.

Standard equipment variations per series were typical. The base models were plain with one sun visor. Mid-price models had a deluxe steering wheel, foam cushions, cigar lighter and power tailgate window on wagons. Top-level cars added carpets, electric clock, back-up lamps (in the center taillamp housing) and full wheel discs.

Chevy's new engine was a 348 ci V-8 with wedge-type cylinder heads. The Turbo-Thrust version was $59.20 extra and a Super Turbo-Thrust edition cost $69.95. Buyers could also get the 283 Turbo-Fire V-8 for $26.90 and Ramjet fuel injection for $484.20, plus a couple of midyear performance engines. New engine mounts, high-pressure cooling and integral-with-block lubrication were improvements.

The 1958 Safety-Girder X-frame formed a backbone for a redesigned underbody with husky cross-members that joined the body to the frame in a new way, permitting lower feature-lines and flatter floors. The front fenders thrust forward to hood the headlamps. The engine hood was extremely low. Rear fenders had a bulge on top, while the sides were contour sculptured to give a gull-wing rear shape.

Two-tone paint ($32.30) could be applied with one color above the entire beltline (either color on roof) and one below, or with one color above the belt toward the front and above the fender contour in the rear (again with roof in either hue). There were seventeen solid colors and thirteen two-tones. Interior trim combinations totaled forty-three. Many used metallic fabrics with imitation leather trim.

Dinah Shore and Pat Boone promoted sales of "longer . . . lower . . . lovelier by far"

1958 Chevys, which came in seventeen models (including sedan delivery). Of interest to collectors are the sporty Impala hardtop and ragtop with their race-car steering wheels and tri-tone upholstery. The Bel Air Sport Coupe is also attractive. A four-door wagon with Bel Air trim took the Nomad name. It featured a liftgate hinged deeply into the roof for extra clearance and a bigger, stronger tailgate with seven vertical chrome trim strips.

For 1959, Chevy introduced its all-new Slimline design with wider, roomier bodies, increased glass area, Spread Wing rear deck styling and large teardrop taillamps. A flat overhang roof was seen on Sport Sedans. Hood ornamentation identified engine type: Chevy script alone on sixes, V with script on 283 ci V-8s and V with script and crossed flag emblem for the 348 ci V-8.

Magic-Mirror finish described a deep-luster acrylic lacquer paint formulated to retain brilliance for years and required less frequent polishing. Drivetrain options started with a lower horsepower six or 185 hp version of the Turbo-Fire 283 ci V-8.

The appearance of the 1958 Chevy interior changed considerably. The new visored instrument panel had wraparound ends. Even Biscaynes had chrome horn ring on steering wheel.

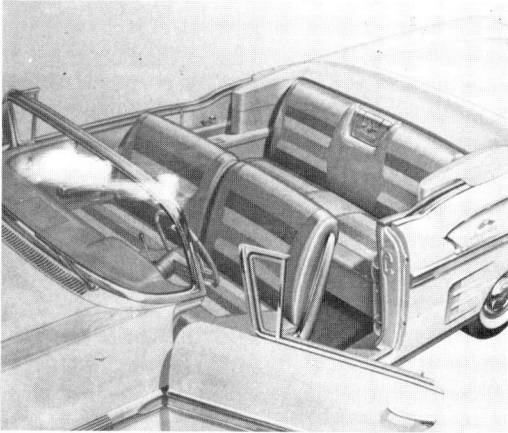

Original artwork for 1958 Chevrolet sales brochure shows the tri-tone interior featured in the Impala convertible. It has seat inserts with wide, horizontal stripes. Note the built-in rear seat radio speaker. *Jack Juratovic Collection*

Chevy's improved brakes had wider, air-cooled drums with twenty-seven percent more bonded area for surer stops. A Corvette donation, the new Muncie four-speed gearbox was controlled via a center-mounted, short-stroke floorshift with gear ratios of 2.20:1 (first), 1.66:1 (second), 1.31:1 (third) and 1.1:1 (fourth).

Body design revisions were eye-catching. The cars had a 1½ in. longer wheelbase, over two additional inches of width, and were about 3 in. lower than comparable 1958s. The hood and front fendertops were flat and shelf-like. Tail fins fanned out in a pair of horizontal curves that looked like a child's drawing of a bird from the rear. The rear deck was extremely long. A compound-curve wraparound windshield was also new. Rear window contours varied according to body style, and headlamps were lowered an amazing 7 in. from 1958.

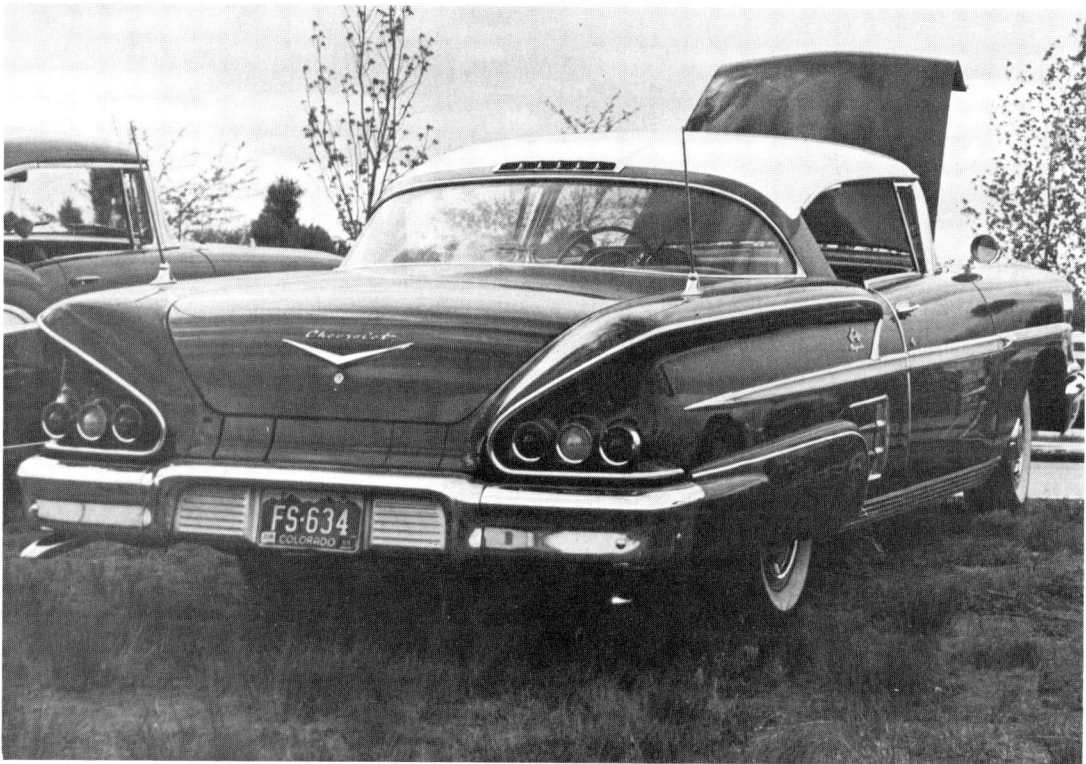

Triple taillamps and simulated air scoop on rear of roof were characteristics of 1958 Bel Airs.

Rear-mounted radio antennas were an option. *Chris Wolfe*

48

Tri-bar wheel covers were standard on 1958 Bel Airs and Impalas. The convertible was offered only in the Bel Air line. Note the four slashes of chrome on front fenders; these were seen on Bel Airs, too.

Bel Airs featured full-length bodyside moldings with white insert in 1959. This is a four-door sedan with V-8 emblem on hood. Cat's-eye openings in front fenders housed parking lamps and directionals. Second color was used on roof and upper rear end.

From a collector's standpoint, the Impala convertible is again the model of choice, followed by the Sport Coupe from the same series. As in 1958, the two-door hardtop had a neat-looking simulated air scoop on the rear edge of the roof. Two body styles not covered in this book—the sedan delivery and the El Camino pickup—are probably next highest on the collectibility list. There was no Bel Air Sport Coupe in 1959 (it returned in 1960), but the flat-top Impala and Bel Air Sport Sedans have some collector appeal, as does the fanciest Nomad.

Chevrolet stressed space, spirit and splendor as selling points of full-size 1960 models. The 1959s proved unsuccessful in the market, but a major revamp was not in the program. So, the 1959 was simply cleaned up and smoothed out to look more refined the following season.

Angular sculpturing replaced the previously curved contours, giving the 1960 models the appearance of being stylized 1959s. Paint colors were more subdued, with choice of pastel-like hues of Suntan Copper, Tasco Turquoise, Jade Green, Cascade Green, Crocus Cream and Sateen Silver. Also popular were Roman Red (especially on convertibles), Tuxedo Black, Royal Blue, Ermine White and Shadow Gray.

Smaller, more conventional round taillamps replaced the large horizontal teardrops of 1959. There was a new Biscayne Fleetmaster sub-series aimed at police departments, taxi companies and other fleet users. A Sport Coupe returned to the Bel Air car line. Big two-door wagons remained among the offerings for their final year.

Engine and transmission options were similar to 1959, with two changes: Ramjet

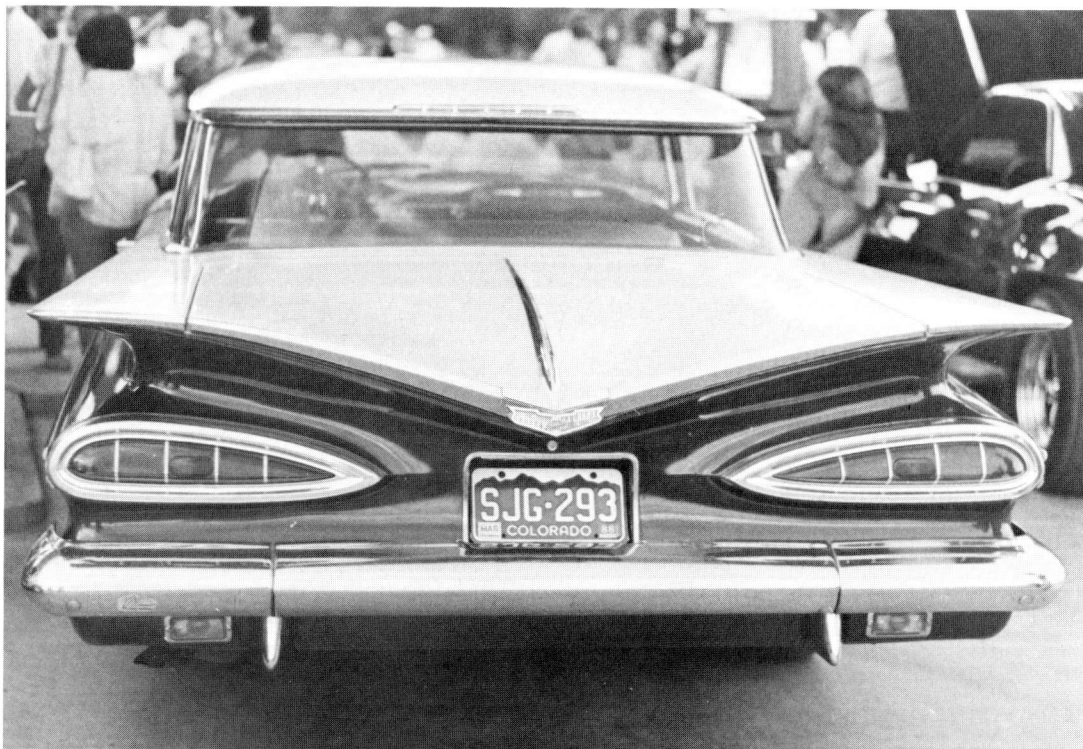

Distinctive gull-wing tail fin styling and teardrop taillights were new for 1959. Impala was the only model to feature vertical chrome moldings on taillights. Back-up lamps were moved to gravel pan below rear bumper. *Chris Wolfe*

fuel injection was no longer offered; and the Special Turbo-Thrust V-8 came only as an 11.25:1 compression job with three two-barrels, high-lift camshaft, solid lifters and dual exhausts. It developed 335 hp at 5800 rpm. Transmission options were also carried over intact.

A few new features were introduced in 1960. The use of Tyrex Cord tires with improved tread was a safety advance for Chevy. The base V-8 also got a new, high-efficiency carburetor. And there were new, larger body mounts and additional sound deadening.

Interiors were revamped to offer what Chevy described as "color-keyed interior beauty . . . a brilliant selection of pattern cloth and leather-grained vinyl upholsteries, floor coverings and tasteful appointments." At car shows today, there's nothing more appealing than a black 1960 Impala with red-and-white-checkered upholstery. Convertibles came with synthetic Cherolon fabric tops, available in four colors, which folded smoothly under a color-coordinated, tailored top boot. Biscaynes now included a cigar lighter, front armrests and dual sun visors at no extra cost.

Ownership

Mechanically, 1958-60 Chevys were pretty good cars. Their biggest service requirement, other than normal maintenance, was front wheel alignment. The 1958 models with V-8s were also prone to a noticeably high incidence of transmission failure, although sixes required less than average transmission repair. Carburetors were an above-average problem on both sixes and V-8s in 1959.

Otherwise, the sixes were about as trouble-free as contemporary Cadillacs. V-8s, however, visited repair shops more frequently. They weren't exceptionally bad, but did need an average amount of fixing, whereas the sixes demanded below-average repairs.

Overall, Chevrolet bodies, regardless of engines, had above-average problems and the sixes were the worst. This probably had to do with the fact that they were purchased by single-car families and saw more hard, everyday use. Among the common areas requiring attention were body noise, rain leaks and rust. Of the three model years, the 1960 models had the fewest body service calls according to owner surveys.

Prospects

In the collector car market, the 1958s show up most frequently and top-condition

The convertible again came only as an Impala in 1959. No rocker panel moldings were seen this year. Rear trim insert could be had in contrasting colors, such as featured on this car, which has more modern tires.

Original art for 1959 Chevrolet sales catalog accurately depicts the convertible interior with plaid seat inserts. Note the special Impala steering wheel with drilled spokes. Side spear shows leaping Impala (behind door edge) decoration and model name in slanted block letters.

51

The Impala Sport Coupe continued to feature a rear-facing scoop on roof. Panoramic rear window improved behind-the-car vision. Rear Chevy emblem followed contour of fins. under it is push-button trunk release mechanism.

As in 1958, Chevy's top-of-the-line station wagon used the Nomad name. As with earlier Nomads, the roof still featured embossed ribs, but now they ran lengthwise on the front section. Tailgate had a lowerable power window. Wagon's taillamps were split in the middle so inner half could lower with tailgate.

The Bel Air offered family sedan room and comfort at a popular price in 1960. Grille and other bright exterior accents were annodized aluminum that resisted rust and corrosion better, but dented easily.

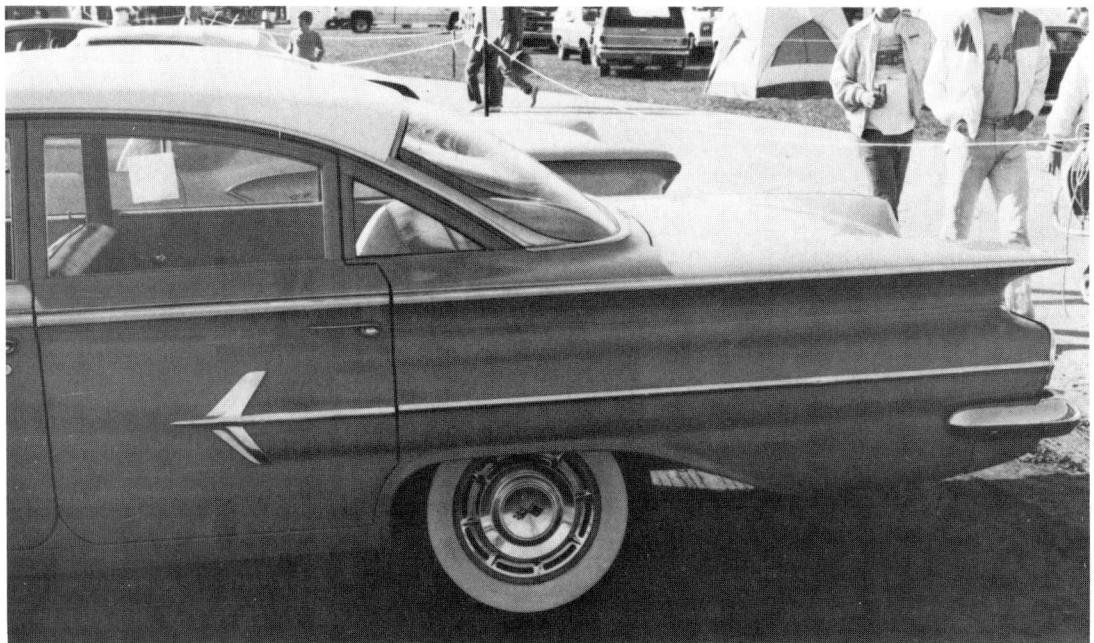

Bel Airs had a simple side molding treatment in 1960. The rear cove (not shown) had a white insert and two taillamps on either side. This is the four-door sedan with extra-cost full wheel covers, which were standard on Impalas.

The 1960 Bel Air interior featured cloth upholstery, vinyl door panels and a twin-spoke steering wheel with horn ring on the bottom. Crank-operated ventipanes, electric wipers, sliding sun visors and high-level cowl ventilation were standard.

convertibles have sold for as high as $43,000. The 1959-60 models are seen more frequently at auctions today, but they don't have the popularity or high prices of the 1958s or the earlier 1955-57 classic Chevys, and probably never will.

Specifications
1958-60 Chevrolet

	1958	1959	1960
Engine	ohv six	ohv six	ohv six
Displacement (ci)	235.5	235.5	235.5
Horsepower (bhp)	145	135	135
Wheelbase (in.)	117½	119	119
Overall length (in.)	209.1	210.9	210.8
Tires (in.)	7.50×14	7.50×14	7.50×14

First seen in 1959, a flat overhanging roofline was used again on 1960 Sport Sedans. Kyle Oberdorf's car shows the Impala rear trim. It's a six, since no V-8 badge is seen below the Chevy emblem on the trunk. Fender skirts were an aftermarket item.

Impalas had four short trim strips on front fendersides in 1960; center portion was painted black. These handsome full wheel discs with knock-off style center insert were extra-cost.

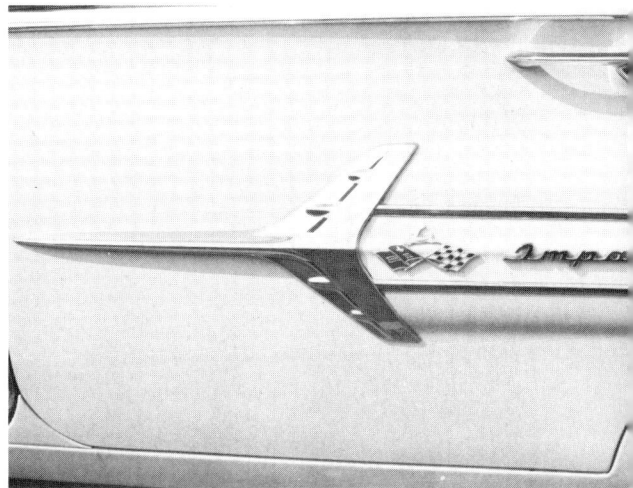

Side trim on 1960 Impalas included wide, double molding treatment with insert, crossed flags and leaping Impala emblem, plus model name-script.

Engines
1958 Chevrolet

Ci	C.R.	Induction	Exhaust	Hp@rpm	Valve lifters
Super Turbo-Fire					
283	9.5	4V	single	230@4800	hydraulic
Turbo-Thrust					
348	9.5	4V	dual	250@4400	hydraulic
Super Turbo-Thrust					
348	9.5	3×2V	dual	280@4800	hydraulic
348	11.0	3×2V	dual	315@5600	solid
Ramjet fuel injection					
283	9.5	FI	single	250@5000	hydraulic
283	10.5	FI	single	290@6200	solid

1959 Chevrolet

Ci	C.R.	Induction	Exhaust	Hp@rpm	Valve lifters
Super Turbo-Fire					
283	9.5	4V	single	230@4800	hydraulic
Ramjet fuel injection					
283	9.5	FI	single	250@5000	hydraulic
283	10.5	FI	single	290@6200	hydraulic
Turbo-Thrust					
348	9.5	4V	dual	250@4400	hydraulic
Super Turbo-Thrust					
348	9.5	3×2V	dual	280@4800	hydraulic
Special Turbo-Thrust					
348	11.0	4V	dual	300@5600	solid
Special Super Turbo-Thrust					
348	11.0	3×2V	dual	315@5600	solid

Production

Fisher style no. 6-cyl	Fisher style no. V-8	Type vehicle
1958 Del Ray		
58-1149	58-1249	4d Sed
58-1141	58-1241	2d Sed
58-1121	58-1221B	2d Utl Sed
58-1171	58-1271	2d Sed D'ly
58-1193	58-1293	4d Sta Wag
58-1191	58-1291	2d Sta Wag
1958 Biscayne		
58-1549	58-1649	4d Sed
58-1541	58-1641	2d Sed
58-1593	58-1693	4d Sta Wag (2S)
58-1594	58-1694	4d Sta Wag (3S)
1958 Bel Air		
58-1749	58-1849	4d Sed
58-1739	58-1839	4d Spt Sed
58-1741	58-1841	2d Sed
58-1731	58-1831	2d Spt Cpe
58-1793	58-1893SD	4d Nomad Wag
1958 Bel Air Impala		
58-1747	58-1847	2d Spt Cpe
58-1767	58-1867	2d Spt Conv

Totals

4d Sedan	491,441
2d Sed	256,182
4d Sta Wag	170,473
Spt Cpe	142.592
Spt Sed	83,330
Conv	55,989
2d Sta Wag	16,590

Source: Jerry Heasley.
Note: Production includes 6-cyl and V-8.

Fisher style no. 6-cyl	Fisher style no. V-8	Type vehicle
1959 Biscayne		
59-1119	59-1219	4d Sed
59-1111	59-1211	2d Sed
59-1121	59-1221	2d Utl Sed
59-1135	59-1235	4d Sta Wag
59-1115	59-1215	2d Sta Wag
1959 Bel Air		
59-1519	59-1619	4d Sed
59-1539	59-1639	4d Spt Sed
59-1511	59-1611	2d Sed
59-1535	59-1635	4d Sta Wag (2S)
59-1545	59-1645	4d Sta Wag (3S)
1959 Impala		
59-1719	59-1819	4d Sed
59-1739	59-1839	4d Spt Sed
59-1737	59-1837	2d Spt Cpe
59-1767	59-1867	2d Conv
59-1735	59-1835	4d Nomad Wag

Totals

4d Sed	525,461
2d Sed	281,924
4d Sta Wag	188,623
Spt Sed	182,520
Spt Cpe	164,901
Conv	72,765
2d Sta Wag	20,760

Source: Jerry Heasley.
Note: Production includes 6-cyl and V-8.

Fisher style no. 6-cyl	Fisher style no. V-8	Type vehicle
1960 Biscayne Fleetmaster		
60-1369	60-1469	4d Sed
60-1311	60-1411	2d Sed
1960 Biscayne		
60-1169	60-1269	4d Sed
60-1111	60-1211	2d Sed
60-1121	60-1221	2d Utl Sed
60-1145	60-1245	4d Sta Wag (3S)
60-1135	60-1235	4d Sta Wag (2S)
1960 Bel Air		
60-1519	60-1619	4d Sed
60-1539	60-1639	4d Spt Sed
60-1511	60-1611	2d Sed
60-1537	60-1637	2d Spt Cpe
60-1545	60-1645	4d Sta Wag (3S)
60-1535	60-1635	4d Sta Wag (2S)
1960 Impala		
60-1719	60-1819	4d Sed
60-1739	60-1839	4d Spt Sed
60-1737	60-1837	2d Spt Cpe
60-1767	60-1867	2d Conv
60-1735	60-1835	4d Nomad Wag

Totals

4d Sed	497,048
2d Sed	228,322
Spt Cpe	204,467
4d Sta Wag	198,066
Spt Sed	169,016
Conv	79,903
2d Sta Wag	14,663

Source: Jerry Heasley.
Note: Production includes 6-cyl and V-8.

Chapter 6

1961-64 Bel Air and Impala

★★★★★	1963 Impala Z-11 Sport Coupe
★★★★★	1962 Impala SS-409 Sport Coupe and convertible
★★★★	1961, 1963, 1964 Impala SS-409 Sport Coupe and convertible
★★★★	1962 Impala SS convertible
★★★★	1962 Bel Air 409 bubble-window two-door sedan
★★★	1962-64 Impala convertible
★★★	1961 Impala SS convertible
★★★	1961-64 Impala SS Sport Coupe
★★	1961-64 Impala and Nomad station wagon
★★	1961-64 Impala Sport Coupe
★	1961-64 Bel Air Sport Coupe
★	1961-64 Impala Sport Sedan

Chevys were trimmer for 1961. New options were the Impala SS package and a handful of 409 ci V-8s. Although another auto maker coined the phrase, "flight deck styling" describes the image of 1961 Chevys. For 1962, feature-lines were more subdued and

Downsized 1961 Chevys continued using easy-to-care-for aluminum trim and had wide expanse of glass for wide-open feeling. Impalas had a wider, tapering side spear with insert and fender ornament.

Chevys grew again. A 327 ci V-8 was new, along with bucket seats and consoles in Super Sports. A crisp, extruded look characterized 1963 models. The cars grew an inch and stressed a luxury image. New for 1963 was a steel cable support for ragtops. About 100 Impala hardtops got a Z-11 drag-racing package before it was banned. Squarish, ultra-clean lines marked the 1964 Chevy's appearance. Super Sports were made a separate series that year.

Serial numbers started with a numeral 1 (1961), 2 (1962), 3 (1963) or 4 (1964) followed by Chevy model number and plant code. New factory codes were: G=Framingham; H=Freemont; R=Arlington; U=Southgate; and Y=Wilmington. Last came the production sequence code.

For quick identification, check front ends. In 1961, the grille had a Chevy emblem and dual headlamps mounted in individual round

This 1961 Impala has optional front bumper guard with black rubber bullets; parking lamps are in opening above headlamps. Clean Sweep parallel action wipers with overlapping pattern were new. Wire wheel covers cost extra.

Solid rear bumper was used on California-built 1961 Chevys and shown in sales catalog. Impala

Sport Coupe had new contoured back window with chrome-trimmed air slots below.

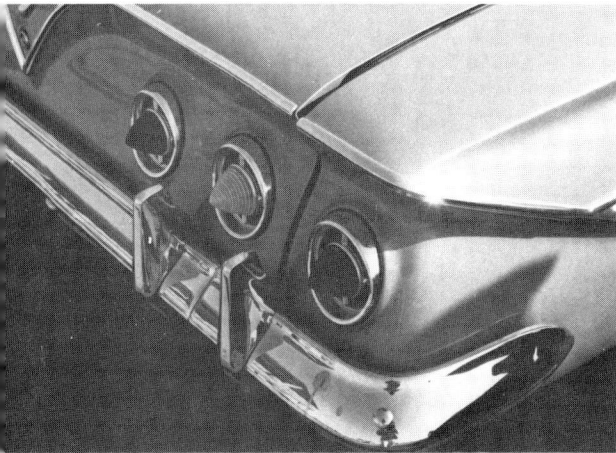

The 1961 instrument cluster was redesigned to put controls in front of driver. Impala steering wheel featured the competition-look. Rich nylon-faced seat upholstery was used inside Impalas, except convertible which had all-vinyl seats.

Impalas had three rear lamps in 1961. The three-piece bumper permitted replacement of individual sections on Snow-Belt cars. Twin guards were standard with this arrangement. V-shaped badge indicating V-8 shows at top left of photo.

housings with parking lamps in the fender tips. The emblem moved above the 1962 grille and headlamps were housed together in a trim panel with parking lamps below. In 1963, the grille was veed horizontally, with headlamps in individual square housings and parking lamps between the housings at the bottom. The 1964 grille had a more horizontal character and rose higher above the headlamps, which were set back in individual round housings. Bumper parking lamps were new that year.

Biscaynes (1961 models) had no side trim. Fleetmaster versions were Spartan with the single sun visor. Others had two visors, foam seats, armrests and glovebox locks. A Biscayne script appeared on the rear fender. Bel Airs used a slightly tapered molding with white inset along the main feature-line, plus an emblem and namescript on rear fenders. Their upholstery was pattern cloth or striped fabric in Sports models. Carpets, automatic dome lamps and deluxe steering wheels were included on Bel Airs. Impalas had wider, fin-shaped feature-line moldings with wide white inserts. A crossed flag emblem and Impala namescript appeared on the trim. Equipment included rich pattern fabrics with vinyl trimmings, three taillights,

electric clock, brake lamp, deep-twist carpets, fingertip door releases and custom length armrests.

The first Super Sport (1961) included SS emblems on the rear fender and deck, special wheel covers, narrow-band whitewalls, power brakes and steering, sintered metallic brakes, tachometer, heavy-duty springs and shocks, dashboard grab bar and chrome housing for cars with four-speed floorshifts. They had 348 or 409 ci V-8s. Only 456 Super Sports were sold in 1961.

Trim variations for 1962 were along the same lines. Bel Airs had a molding along the upper beltline. The molding had a color insert on Impalas, which also had three taillights and silver annodized rear panel finish. The SS option added emblems, bucket seats, console and other goodies like all-vinyl monochromatic interiors.

Bodyside trim for 1963 was lacking on Biscaynes, while Bel Airs had a thin molding along the lower feature-line. Impalas had a wider molding with a white swirl-pattern insert. Again, Impalas had silver annodized rear panels and triple taillights. Impala emblems showed a leaping Impala in a circle of chrome on the rear fenders, with SS letters added on Super Sports.

Lower car lines were trimmed basically the same in 1964, however, a Super Sport series was added. Impalas had a wide molding with a white insert around the upper edges of the rear body panel. SS features included leather-grained vinyl upholstery, bucket seats, console, swirl-pattern instrument panel inserts, SS emblems, silver annodized rear finish and full wheel covers of special design.

To be a wise buyer of early 1960s Chevys, you have to know how to read engine charts and understand the drag-racing, high-performance world. A 409 ci engine can have a big effect on the value of such cars.

Only 142 of the 409 ci V-8s were installed in 1961 Chevys, but the 348 jobs performed well since the cars were downsized from 1960 (though on the same wheelbase). The smaller bodies were lighter in weight, which enhanced performance. Also, the frame was changed to a conventional perimeter type that improved ride stability, roadability and handling.

Initially, Chevy went into the 1961 market with the six and a couple of mild 283 ci V-8s, plus four-barrel (340 hp) and triple-carburetor (350 hp) versions of the 348. The midyear 409 was a bored and stroked modification of the big-block. It had a single four-barrel and 360 hp.

For 1962, the base V-8 was a 170 hp two-barrel on the 283 ci block. Options on a new 327 ci block included 250 hp and 300 hp Turbo-Fire engines, both with single four-barrels and dual exhaust. The 409 had become a regular production option in two Turbo-Fire versions: 380 hp with solid lifters, high-lift cam and dual exhaust or the all-out 409 hp edition with one horse per cubic inch. This engine had the solid lifters with dual quad carburetion and special light-weight valvetrain.

More power was offered in 1963. The six had less cubes, but five more horses, while the base 283 was raised to 195 hp. Options for the 327 ci block included 250 hp and 300 hp. The 409 came in a new, milder 340 hp setup, but there were also 400 hp and 425 hp editions. The early-in-the-year Z-11 was king of the high-performance hill, however. It was primarily a Super Stock drag-racing package with aluminum front end parts, a sound insulation deletion and a stroked version of the big V-8 that displaced 427 ci and developed 430 hp. (A Mystery 427 with angled-valve porcupine heads was also developed for the NASCAR superspeedways, but not available in regular cars.)

Approximately 100 cars with the Z-11 kit were made before General Motors banned factory participation in racing during the fall

Factory-type 1962 Chevy tachometer had the look of an add-on item. It's seen here on a 409 powered Bel Air. Underdash gauge package was an extra.

Cars with base 283 ci V-8s had V-shaped emblem with numeral 8 call-out, but no crossed flags. Emblem is for the 409 ci big-block. These hubcaps were standard on Bel Airs.

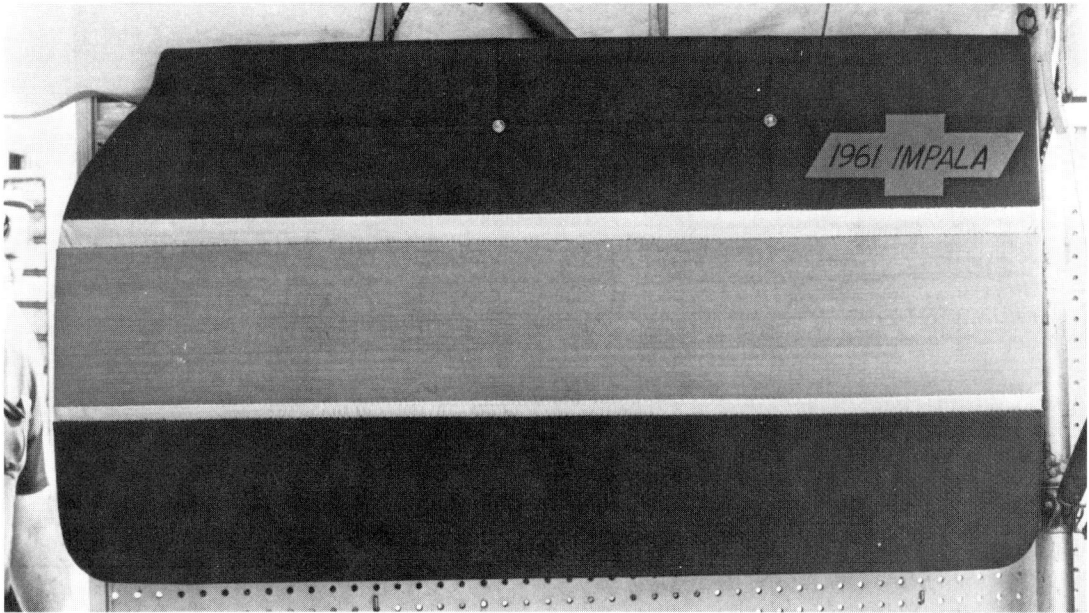

CARS, Incorporated, of Berkley, Michigan, sells reproduction door panels for 1961s. Impalas also had full carpeting and vinyl headliner, which CARS can supply.

Crossed flags on the front fender of 1962 Chevy convertible at James Leake's Tulsa, Oklahoma, auction indicate it has the 409 ci engine. These wide whitewalls are wider than original type.

Detail shows rear of 1962 Impala ragtop with three-piece rear bumper. Impala shared alumi- nized cove finish with Bel Air, but had a horizontal molding between triple taillamps.

of 1963. Production of both 427 V-8s was halted immediately. The ban also inspired Chevy to adopt a holding pattern in the performance market; consequently the 1964 engines were virtually identical to those of 1963.

Ownership

According to owner surveys, all 1961-64 Chevys had an above-average number of complaints of rattles. In addition, wheel alignment was a standout problem on V-8s. The 1963-64 V-8s also went to the shop more than usual for transmission fixes. The same was true for the 1961 and 1963 V-8 carburetors and mufflers on 1961-62 sixes and 1962 and 1964 V-8s. In general, sixes held up a little better than V-8s concerning repairs, but all Chevys required a lot more fixing than Plymouths and Dodges of the same years, and only slightly more than counterpart Fords. These survey results

have little to do with current collectibility, however. Demand and prices for Chevys today are higher than for Mopars or Fords.

Prospects

In auctions, Impalas dominate the list of non-Corvette Chevys (1961-64) crossing the block. Slightly over half of 1987 consignments had the SS option. The non-SS model of choice is the ragtop, but nearly all 1961-63 Super Sports in 1987 auctions were hardtops. With the 1964 models, this moves in favor of hardtops.

Experts say the rare 1961 SS is least popular as an investment, since NOS (new-old-stock) parts are hard to find and few repros (reproduction parts) are available. This keeps demand down, as restoration is so costly. Yet, the highest price paid in 1987 for cars of these years was $22,000 for a '62 Impala convertible. A second such car in the same condition, however, sold for half as much at another auction.

Dual taillamp treatment was a 1962 Bel Air trademark. This 409 powered Sport Coupe has one-piece rear bumper. Bel Air name is on rear fenders. Upholstery in this car is incorrect.

Most popular is the 1964 Super Sport, although for these models the supply factor is high enough to keep top prices for SS convertibles at $13,000. So, experts say the 1962 Impala SS ragtop with the 409 engine takes the cake as the top investment—it best

Full wheel covers for 1962 had a bright and attractive appearance. They were standard on Impalas, optional otherwise. Whitewalls were narrower and this style is correct for car.

represents the 409 legend. It's hard, but not impossible, to find, and parts can be obtained. Even without the 409, these cars are bringing up to $15,000 today.

As for 1963s, the Impala SS ragtops are currently hitting peak prices of $14,000. Parts are available, so the cars are about as good an investment as 1961s and 1964s. They haven't quite caught up with the 1962s, however. An exception is the Z-11, because any factory lightweight Super Stocker—Chevy, Ford, Pontiac, Dodge—is a top-dollar investment in today's market.

Buyers of 1961 models should check the condition of side trim; it's hard and expensive to replace. Taillight trim is the big problem with 1962s. It's usually damaged and extremely difficult to find. Side moldings don't hold up well on 1963s either, especially on Super Sports. Lower grille moldings for all 1964 Chevys are a restorer's nightmare. Two common problems on all these cars are bad padded dashboards and rust in the floor pan or frame. I know of one 1963 ragtop that looks perfect, but has so much frame rustout that the front wheels are ready to fall off.

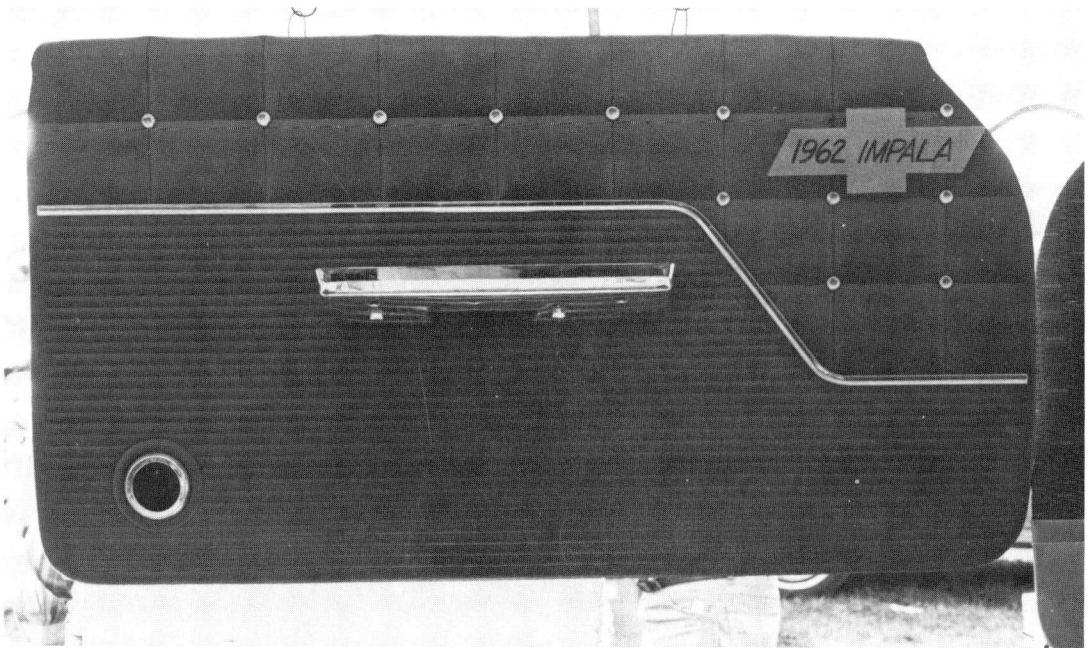

CARS specializes in 1955-72 Chevrolet interior kits. This is the 1962 Impala door panel the company sells. Reflector on lower left alerts oncoming cars when door is opened.

Low-mileage 1963 Bel Air two-door sedan with six-cylinder engine showed up at the fall 1988 Carlisle Car Corral. It could be a high-performance car with 409 engine.

Pointed front and rear fenderlines character-ized 1963 big-car styling. Impalas had front fenderside decorations, wider feature-line mold-ing with insert and leaping Impala in chrome circle emblem on rear fenders. *Chris Wolfe*

Optional 1961 V-8s included the Super Turbo-Fire 348 ci engine with 280 hp, as seen here on a car with 20,000 original miles.

Base V-8 for 1961 was the Turbo-Fire 283 cubic incher. Economy version came with a two-barrel and 170 hp. Super Turbo-Fire version had a four-barrel and 230 hp rating.

On 1963 Super Sports, the circle on rear fenders had SS emblems; aluminized cove and triple taillamps remained trademarks of Impalas.

Pencil-stripe whitewalls on this convertible are not like original type, but look good. *Chris Wolfe*

All-vinyl upholstery highlights the interior of 1964 convertible. The car owned by Rod and Mary Ryan of Green Bay, Wisconsin, is a convertible with factory in-dash tachometer. It's a non-SS Impala with three-on-the-tree gearshifting.

The 1964 Chevys continued to feature crisp, extruded styling, but had boxier fender contours. This Impala station wagon is V-8 powered and has the standard full wheel discs.

Impala Sport Coupe had the look of a convertible at rear of roof. Thin chrome moldings on side and rear repeated the rectangular styling theme. V-8 emblems appear on front fender.

Model name and leaping Impala circle (SS circle on Super Sports) were part of top series' trim package. *Chevrolet Motor Division*

Specifications
1961-64 Chevrolet

	1961	1962	1963	1964
Engine	ohv six	ohv six	ohv six	ohv six
Displacement (ci)	235.5	235.5	230	230
Horsepower (bhp)	135	135	140	140
Wheelbase (in.)	119	119	119	119
Overall length (in.)	209.3	—	210.4	209.9
Tires (in.)	7.50×14	7.50×14	7.00×14	7.00×14

Engines
1961-64 Chevrolet

Year	Ci	Bore×stroke	Bhp@rpm	Torque@rpm	Induction
1962-63	327	4.00×3.25	340@6000	344@4000	4V
1961	348	4.13×3.25	340@5800	362@3600	3×2V
1961	348	4.13×3.25	350@6000	365@3600	3×2V
1961	409	4.31×3.50	360@5800	409@3600	4V
1961-62	409	4.31×3.50	380@5800	420@3600	4V
1963-64	409	4.31×3.50	400@5800	425@3600	4V
1961-62	409	4.31×3.50	409@6000	420@4000	2×4V
1963-64	409	4.31×3.50	425@6000	425@4200	2×4V
1963	427	4.40×3.50	430@6000	430@4000	2×4V

Performance
1961-64 Chevrolet

Year/model	Ci/Bhp	0-60 mph	¼ mile
'61 Bel Air Spt Cpe (Comp)	409/409	—	12.83 sec
'61 Impala SS HT	409/360	7.8 sec	15.8
'62 Impala SS HT	409/409	6.3	14.9
'63 Impala SS HT	327/340	6.6	15.2
'64 Impala SS HT	409/400	7.5	15.3

Production

Fisher style no. 6-cyl	Fisher style no. V-8	Type vehicle
1961 Biscayne Fleetmaster		
61-1369	61-1469	4d Sed
61-1311	61-1411	2d Sed
1961 Biscayne		
61-1169	61-1269	4d Sed
61-1111	61-1211	2d Sed
61-1121	61-1221	2d Utl Sed
61-1145	61-1245	4d Sta Wag (3S)
61-1135	61-1235	4d Sta Wag (2S)
1961 Bel Air		
61-1569	61-1669	4d Sed
61-1539	61-1639	4d Spt Sed
61-1511	61-1611	2d Sed
61-1537	61-1637	2d Spt Cpe
61-1545	61-1645	4d Sta Wag (3S)
61-1535	61-1635	4d Sta Wag (2S)
1961 Impala		
61-1769	61-1869	4d Sed
61-1739	61-1839	4d Spt Sed
61-1711	61-1811	2d Sed
61-1737	61-1837	2d Spt Cpe
61-1767	61-1867	2d Conv
61-1745	61-1845	4d Sta Wag (3S)
61-1735	61-1835	4d Sta Wag (2S)

Totals

4d Sed	452,251
Spt Cpe	177,969
Spt Sed	174,141
4d Sta Wag	168,935
2d Sed	153,988
Conv	64,624

Source: Jerry Heasley.
Note: Production includes 6-cyl and V-8.

Fisher style no. 6-cyl	Fisher style no. V-8	Type vehicle
1962 Biscayne		
62-1169	62-1269	4d Sed
62-1111	62-1211	2d Sed
62-1135	62-1235	4d Sta Wag
1962 Bel Air		
62-1569	62-1669	4d Sed
62-1511	62-1611	2d Sed
62-1537	62-1637	2d Spt Cpe
62-1545	62-1645	4d Sta Wag (3S)
62-1535	62-1635	4d Sta Wag (2S)

Fisher style no. 6-cyl	Fisher style no. V-8	Type vehicle
1962 Impala		
62-1769	62-1869	4d Sed
62-1739	62-1839	4d Spt Sed
62-1747	62-1847	2d Spt Cpe
62-1767	62-1867	2d Conv
62-1745	62-1845	4d Sta Wag (3S)
62-1735	62-1835	4d Sta Wag (2S)
Totals		
4d Sed		533,349
Spt Cpe		323,427
4d Sta Wag		187,566
Spt Sed		176,077
2d Sed		127,870
Conv		75,719

Source: Jerry Heasley.
Note: *Production includes 6-cyl and V-8.*

Fisher style no. 6-cyl	Fisher style no. V-8	Type vehicle
1963 Biscayne		
63-1169	63-1269	4d Sed
63-1111	63-1211	2d Sed
63-1135	63-1235	4d Sta Wag (2S)
1963 Bel Air		
63-1569	63-1669	4d Sed
63-1511	63-1611	2d Sed
63-1545	63-1645	4d Sta Wag (3S)
63-1535	63-1635	4d Sta Wag (2S)
1963 Impala		
63-1769	63-1869	4d Sed
63-1739	63-1839	4d Spt Sed
63-1747	63-1847	2d Spt Cpe
63-1767	63-1867	2d Conv
63-1745	63-1845	4d Sta Wag (3S)
63-1735	63-1835	4d Sta Wag (2S)
Totals		
4d Sed		516,511
Spt Cpe		399,224
Spt Sed		198,542
4d Sta Wag		194,158
2d Sed		135,636
Conv		82,659

Source: Jerry Heasley.
Note: *Production includes 6-cyl and V-8.*

Fisher style no. 6-cyl	Fisher style no. V-8	Type vehicle
1964 Biscayne		
64-1169	64-1269	4d Sed
64-1111	64-1211	2d Sed
64-1135	64-1235	4d Sta Wag (2S)
1964 Bel Air		
64-1569	64-1669	4d Sed
64-1511	64-1611	2d Sed
64-1535	64-1635	4d Sta Wag (2S)
64-1545	64-1645	4d Sta Wag (3S)
1964 Impala		
64-1769	64-1869	4d Sed
64-1739	64-1839	4d Spt Sed
64-1747	64-1847	2d Spt Cpe
64-1767	64-1867	2d Conv
64-1735	64-1835	4d Sta Wag (2S)
64-1745	64-1845	4d Sta Wag (3S)
1964 Impala SS		
64-1347	64-1447	2d Spt Cpe
64-1367	64-1467	2d Conv
Totals		
4d Sed		536,329
Spt Cpe		442,292
Spt Sed		200,172
Sta Wag		192,827
2d Sed		120,951
Conv		81,897

Source: Jerry Heasley.
Note: *Production includes 6-cyl and V-8.*

Chapter 7

1965-70 Impala and Caprice

★★★★★	1965 Impala SS convertible (with 409 or 396)
★★★★★	1967-69 Impala SS-427 convertible
★★★★	1966 Impala SS convertible (with 427 or 396)
★★★★	1965 Impala SS Sport Coupe (with 409 or 396)
★★★★	1970 Impala SS-454 convertible
★★★★	1967-69 Impala SS-427 Sport Coupe
★★★	1965-70 Impala SS convertible
★★★	1966 Impala SS Sport Coupe (with 397 or 396)
★★★	1966-70 Caprice coupe
★★	1967-70 Impala SS Sport Coupe
★★	1965-70 Impala convertible
★	1965-70 Impala Sport Coupe
★	1966 Caprice station wagon
★	1970 Impala Custom Coupe

Larger restyled Chevys appeared in 1965. Fastback rooflines, Turbo Hydramatic transmission and a midyear Caprice luxury sedan were new. A formal-roof Caprice coupe was added along with a 1966 facelift. Also new was the wood-trimmed Caprice wagon. The base engine for 1965 was upped to a 250 ci six. Of collector interest for 1967 Chevys

The 1965 Chevys had more fluid lines and Coke-bottle feature-lines. Deep grille styling was split horizontally by front bumper bar. This non-SS Sport Coupe has optional simulated wire wheel covers.

Triple taillamps again identified Impalas in 1965. Sport Coupe has new fastback roofline. Trim was simpler than in previous season, giving a cleaner overall appearance.

was the SS-427 model option and new fluid body sculpturing. In 1968, the Impala added a Custom Coupe with notchback roofline to complement the fastback. The SS-427 remained a low-production item. Concealed headlamps, hidden windshield wipers and a base 307 ci V-8 were introduced.

Big Chevys were totally redesigned for 1969. They grew longer and had integrated

The 1965 Impala SS interior had distinctive door panels with SS identification. Bucket seats and console with gauge and SS emblem were optional. This convertible has automatic transmission with T-handle floor shifter and optional power windows.

Impala Sport Coupe interior for 1965 featured pattern cloth upholstery. This car has standard three-speed manual transmission with column shifter. Woodgrain trim on lower dash was a non-SS Impala feature.

bumper grilles, ventless side windows and anti-theft steering columns. The 327 was reinstated as the standard V-8. A more conventional grille, facelifted bodies and new 400 and 454 ci engines were seen in 1970.

Beginning in 1965, serial numbers were moved to the top left-hand side of the instrument panel. The vehicle identification number (VIN) consisted of thirteen symbols beginning with a numeral 1 for Chevrolet, then the model number. The sixth symbol was the last digit of the model year (5=1965, and so on), followed by a manufacturing plant code. The last six digits were the sequential vehicle number, starting at 100,001.

Appearancewise, the 1965 and 1966 Chevys look similar. The 1965 has a front emblem and grille parking lamps. In 1966, parking lamps were built into the bumper. Small, round taillights in 1965 contrasted to the 1966's large, horizontal lenses. The torpedoshaped 1967s had front fender-tip ornaments that resembled the grille, while 1968s had parking lamps in the fender tips and flared wheelhousings. Some 1968 Caprices had optional hideaway headlamps. The 1969 models are easy to spot with their integral bumper grille. In 1970, the grille is

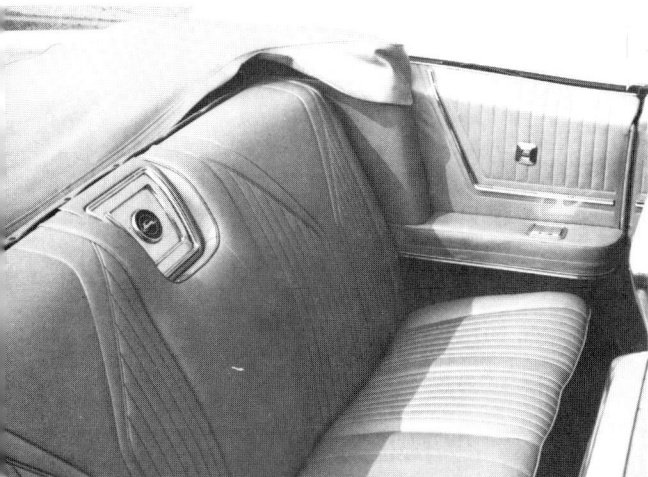

Rear seat of 1965 Impala convertible featured all-vinyl trim and leaping Impala logo at upper center. Top boot was color-coordinated vinyl. Power windows are an extra that collectors like.

Chrome Super Sport signature appears on front fender of 1966 SS models. Cars with base 283 ci engine had V-8 badge, no displacement call-out. SS wheel covers had tri-bar center insert.

more conventional and the recessed vertical-slot taillamps in the bumper are a telltale sign of that year.

Biscaynes, Bel Airs and Impalas were offered all six years. The Caprice started as a Sport Sedan option in mid-1965 and became a full series thereafter. An SS series was offered until 1968, when it reverted to option status. The SS-427 had all SS goodies, plus special call-out badges, red-stripe tires, disc brakes, heavy-duty suspension, 15 in. wheels and special hood with decorative simulated air vents.

During this period, the less expensive cars' equipment kept growing, while model

This 1966 Impala four-door sedan has front bumper guard added. Lower portion of grille showing below bumper was narrower than 1965 style. V-8 front fender badge has 327 displacement call-out.

Back-up lamps were moved into 1966 bumper. Robert Moses' car has the three-piece bumper, which no longer came with bumper guards standard. A chrome bar with Impala SS name appears under Chevrolet signature. Rear mount antenna was a popular option.

Caprice started as an Impala trim option in mid-1965 and this new Caprice Custom Coupe was introduced for 1966. It had a more formal roof-line and body pinstriping.

Chevy's 1966 taillamps came in many styles. Shown clockwise from upper left are Caprice Custom lens with chrome moldings; Chevy II lens; standard Chevy lens (note one-piece bumper); Corvair taillamps; "tunneled" Corvette lenses; and Chevelle SS version.

Impala SS for 1967 had grille styling emphasizing horizontal bars, with black-out finish between them. This convertible has insignia for 327 ci V-8 on front fender. Same wheel covers were seen on all Impalas, but with SS center inserts on Super Sports.

Taillamps for 1967 again had triple segmented horizontal styling, but no longer wrapped around body corners. Dual exhausts indicate a high-performance V-8 powers this non-SS Impala.

The 1967 Chevys had car-of-the-future styling and rounder, more massive lines. This non-SS Impala convertible has crossed flags and 396 front fender call-outs.

Super Sports had Impala SS nameplate on left side of grille. Bumper guards were optional. Parking lamps and directional signals were in narrow bumper slot. The three-segment auxiliary marker lamps with white lens could be ordered to replace regular grille corners.

Non-SS Impala wheel covers used centers with bow-tie, while Super Sport had same covers with SS center inserts. These whitewalls are very close to factory-issue type. The V-8 emblem seen here indicates 396 Turbo-Jet engine is used.

Here's the 1967 Impala SS showing a close-up of the badge used to call out the 327 ci V-8 engine. Another option was the Turbo-Jet 427 powerplant, in which case a much larger 427 call-out appeared above crossed flags. Party Hat hub centers indicate disc brakes.

Factory photo promotes new-for-1967 eight-track solid state stereo player option. Caprice interior with wood trim is also nicely illustrated. Getting eight-track tapes isn't easy today.

options like the Super Sport were gradually downgraded. By 1970, the Biscayne came with carpets, full safety equipment and a couple of bright window moldings. Meanwhile, the SS (now optional) had changed from a true performance car option to merely a bucket seat option with little more than the SS name badge. Bucket seats and a console became individual options. Biscaynes remained plain looking, without body-side moldings. Bel Airs had full-length moldings and richer vinyl and pattern cloth trims. Impalas sported more window dressing, full wheel discs, rocker panel moldings, deluxe steering wheel and triple unit taillamps.

Caprices were essentially fancy Impalas with distinctive side moldings, extra chrome, electric clock, woodgrained dashes and armrest seats in knit nylon and vinyl or brocade cloth and vinyl. In some years, there was a Caprice SS-427 with options like bucket seats, Rally wheels, pencil-stripe

Styling for 1968 was softened. Here's a non-SS Impala convertible. Rectangular side-marker lamps, by then standard, had engine call-outs (327 shown). Wire wheel covers were optional.

tires and floor-mounted manual gearshift. The hot Caprices were a favorite of road testers and turned in some good performance.

Ownership

Chevys built from 1965 to 1970 were still pretty much average-rated cars in owner surveys. The 1965-66 models, which today seem to be the most collectible of the group, were the worst mechanically. The main problems were rattles (on both sixes and V-8s), plus above-average need for wheel alignments on V-8s. The 1965 also had more than normal rust affliction and muffler replacement rates. Almost everything else was just average. In other words, there was nothing outstandingly bad or good about the 1965-66 models. In contrast, Chrysler products of the period required far fewer repairs. Ford, however, had slumped somewhat, and came out about the same as Chevy on surveys. *Consumer Reports* classed 1965-66 Chevy sixes and V-8s as undesirable.

The cars got a middle-of-the-road rating on road tests, too. Accommodations, ride quality, handling, braking, steering and performance were all appraised as good to fair, but the two-speed automatic transmission was described as "not versatile" and the high repair rate kept the overall rating of sixes and V-8s low. In fact, surveys showed heavy transmission problems in 1965, which might be why Turbo Hydramatic was phased-in late that year.

Chevy must have made some product improvements though, since the 1967-70 models came out a bit better on surveys. In fact, they even had a few strong points: good engines and drivelines, better than average brakes and body hardware and slightly improved exhaust systems and shocks. However, collectors might be interested in the Chevy's shortcomings in exterior finish and body integrity. They were prone to rust, especially in the rear quarter panels.

Overall the frequency of repairs remained fairly high. Mopar cars and Fords (except Mercurys) slipped in quality as well and did noticeably worse than Chevys on 1967-70 repair surveys. Thus Chevy's modest improvement probably meant a lot in the new-car marketplace.

On the other hand, Chevy did provide an exceptionally good ride and handling package, good brakes (with power front discs) and comfortable seating. The air conditioning system was also highly rated. The Stovebolt six could, however, be a bit balky when it was cold.

Prospects

In the current collector market, among Chevys of the six-year period the 1965 models are the top prize. They are proving to be so desirable among hobbyists that reproduction parts are already available to restorers, which isn't true for post-1965 models. Surprisingly, the 1966 models aren't nearly as popular, with the exception of the Caprice coupes. The first two-door Caprice is coming on strong as a future collectible, especially in big-engined, heavily optioned format.

Today the 1965 Impala SS models and 1966 Caprice coupes look like excellent investments, but not because they're already bringing high prices. This isn't the case. In 1987, the top dollar paid for a 1965 was $6,400; that's about twenty percent higher than the average for basically sound cars. During the first half of 1988, however, the number of 1965s for sale and the asking and

Chrome dress-up package brightened up the appearance of the high-performance 396 ci 375 hp Turbo-Jet V-8 engine.

Dave Ehler's 1968 Impala Custom Coupe shows off new rear end styling. With return to triple round taillamps, the lenses found their way into the bumper for the first time.

These are 1968 Rally wheels without disc brakes, although the small hubcaps used look similar to Party Hats. Upper belt molding has vinyl protective insert. This is an Impala Custom Coupe, as indicated by nameplate on fender below script.

Chevrolet name was on hood on 1969 Impalas and Caprice Customs. This car has rare fender-mounted turn indicators. *Chris Wolfe*

For 1969, front side-markers stood on end, but still had engine call-outs (327 shown). Caprice and Impala Custom Coupes had formal roof that went great with vinyl top. This is the Impala.

selling prices on them have both been spiraling upward as the supply of older postwar Chevys diminishes. The writing is on the wall—a great opportunity for short-term investing exists in the market right now. Therefore, I've allotted three, four and five-star investment ratings to the rarest of these cars.

In contrast, the number of 1967-70 Chevys being traded drops off substantially, although prices are relatively strong on what is changing hands. These are primarily the big-engined Super Sports and Caprices, particularly the SS-427s, which were sold in small numbers. However, it's relatively easy to forge one from a regular Impala SS, so insist on documentation of the car's history when considering such a purchase.

Other cars of interest (not necessarily high value) are the original 1965½ Caprice Sport Sedans, the low-production six-cylinder Super Sports (400 made in 1967, but probably not a very good investment), Caprice station wagons with lots of options (like a 427) and—very collectible—mint orig-

inal Biscayne two-door sedans with 396 and 427 ci engines and stick shift. These were built essentially as off-the-line racing cars, as the big-block could do its stuff best in the lighter weight Biscayne coupe. Some stripped-down wagons with big-block V-8s were also ordered out by drag racers because their weight bias made them quick out of the chutes. As you can see, high-performance wasn't totally dead yet, and the real quarter-mile machines can be good investments, regardless of trim level or body style.

Beyond high-performance engines, 1965-70 Chevy collectors are looking at body styles, appearance options and factory accessories. It's hard to lose with a convertible . . . when the top goes down, the price goes up. The next most popular model is the Sport Coupe; both fastback and notchback editions are popular. Some experts like the notchback Custom Coupes best and believe that Sport Sedans and wagons will catch on later. Extras to look for are bucket seats, consoles, floorshifts, air conditioning and vinyl tops.

Tim Streblow's 1969 Caprice Custom Sport Sedan featured sophisticated looking wheel covers. Other standard Caprice Custom additions included brocade upholstered seats and wood interior trim.

Styled much like its Caprice counterpart, the 1969 Impala Sport Sedan has model-name signatures on front fenders. Lack of engine call-out indicates this is a six-cylinder Chevy.

Impalas in 1970 had front fender signatures for identification. This ragtop has 400 ci V-8 call-out near front. Full wheel covers were standard on Impalas; twin-stripe whitewalls were new.

Grille design for 1970 had a mid-1960s look. The base-level Biscayne sedan had its name on front fender. Rear side-markers were larger and vertically segmented. *Chevrolet Motor Division*

Tim Streblow's 1970 Impala Sport Sedan has base 350 ci V-8. Fender skirts were included with Caprice Custom package, optional otherwise; mag-style wheel covers extra. *Tim Streblow*

Taillamps stayed in 1970 bumper, but adopted vertical-rectangular shape. Dual exhausts indicate Tim Streblow's 350 is the four-barrel version. Rear antenna was still available. *Tim Streblow*

Specifications
1965-70 Chevrolet

	1965	1966	1967	1968	1969	1970
Engine	ohv six	ohv six	ohv six	ohv six	ohv six	ohv six
Displacement (ci)	230	250	250	250	250	250
Horsepower (bhp)	140	155	155	155	155	155
Wheelbase (in.)	119	119	119	119	119	119
Overall length (in.)	213.1	213.2	213.2	215	216	216
Tires (in.)	7.35×14	7.35×14	8.25×14	8.25×14	8.25×14	F78×15

Engines
1965-70 Chevrolet

Type	Bore×stroke	Ci	Bhp
1965			
6	3.88×3.25	230	140
V-8	3.87×3.00	283	195
V-8	4.00×3.25	327	250
V-8	4.09×3.76	396	325
V-8	4.09×3.76	396	425
V-8	4.31×3.50	427	340
V-8	4.31×3.50	427	400
1966			
6	3.88×3.53	250	155
V-8	3.87×3.00	283	195
V-8	4.00×3.25	327	275
V-8	4.09×3.76	396	325
V-8	4.31×3.50	427	390
V-8	4.31×3.50	427	425

Engines
1965-70 Chevrolet

Type	Bore×stroke	Ci	Bhp
1967			
6	3.88×3.53	250	155
V-8	3.87×3.00	283	195
V-8	4.00×3.25	327	275
V-8	4.09×3.76	396	325
V-8	4.31×3.50	427	385
V-8	4.31×3.50	427	425
1968			
6	3.88×3.53	250	155
V-8	3.88×3.25	307	200
V-8	4.00×3.25	327	250
V-8	4.00×3.25	327	275
V-8	4.09×3.76	396	325
V-8	4.31×3.50	427	385
V-8	4.31×3.50	427	425

Unrestored engine compartment on Tim Streblow's 1970 Impala houses small-block 350 base V-8. Emission controls now played a larger role in car engineering. *Tim Streblow*

Woodgrained steering wheel and dashboard were standard in 1970 Impalas. Most engine monitoring was handled by idiot lights.

Engines
1965-70 Chevrolet

Type	Bore×stroke	Ci	Bhp
1969			
6	3.88×3.53	250	155
V-8	4.00×3.25	327	235
V-8	4.00×3.48	350	255
V-8	4.00×3.48	350	300
V-8	4.09×3.76	396	265
V-8	4.31×3.50	427	335
V-8	4.31×3.50	427	390

Engines
1965-70 Chevrolet

Type	Bore×stroke	Ci	Bhp
1970			
6	3.88×3.53	250	155
V-8	4.00×3.48	350	250
V-8	4.00×3.48	350	300
V-8	4.13×3.76	400	265
V-8	4.25×4.00	454	345
V-8	4.25×4.00	454	390

Note: Engine families for 1965-70 were Turbo-Thrift (6-cyl), Turbo-Fire (small-block V-8) and Turbo-Jet (big-block V-8).

Performance
1965-70 Chevrolet

Year/model	Ci/Bhp	0-60 mph	¼ mile
1965 Caprice Sport Sedan	396/325	8.4 sec	16.5 sec
1965 Caprice Sport Coupe	427/400	7.9	15.5
1967 Impala SS Sport Coupe	427/385	8.4	15.8
1969 Caprice Custom Coupe	427/390	7.7	15.5 (90 mph)
1970 Impala wagon (modified)	427/390	—	13.41 (103.68 mph)

The 1970 Caprice coupe came standard with 350 ci V-8. Options included the 400 V-8 and 454 big-block, which is most desired by collectors. Wheel covers were of new design for 1970.

Production

Model no.	Fisher style no.	Type vehicle
1965 Biscayne		
153/154	15369	4d Sed
153/154	15311	2d Sed
153/154	15335	4d Sta Wag (2S)
1965 Bel Air		
155/156	15569	4d Sed
155/156	15511	2d Sed
155/156	15535	4d Sta Wag (2S)
155/156	15536	4d Sta Wag (3S)
1965 Impala		
163/164	16369	4d Sed
163/164	16337	2d HT Cpe
163/164	16339	4d Spt Sed
163/164	16367	2d Conv
163/164	16335	4d Sta Wag (2S)
163/164	16345	4d Sta Wag (3S)
1965 Impala Super Sport		
165/166	16537	2d Spt Cpe
165/166	16567	2d Conv
Totals		
Spt Cpe		558,459
4d Sed		480,801
Spt Sed		252,048
4d Sta Wag		184,316
2d Sed		99,188
Conv		72,760

Source: Jerry Heasley.

Note: Production includes 6-cyl and V-8.

Model no.	Fisher style no.	Type vehicle
1966 Impala SS		
167/168	16737	2d Spt Cpe
167/168	16767	2d Conv
1966 Caprice		
166	16639	4d Spt Sed
166	16647	2d Spt Cpe
166	16645	4d Sta Wag (3S)
166	16635	4d Sta Wag
Totals		
Biscayne six		83,200
Biscayne V-8		39,200
Bel Air six		72,100
Bel Air V-8		164,500
Impala six		33,100
Impala V-8		621,800
Impala SS		119,300
Caprice		181,000

Source: Standard Catalog of American Cars 1946-1975.

Note: Fisher style no. shown for 6-cyl; production includes 6-cyl and V-8. Caprice and Impala SS were V-8-only models. Production totals rounded off to nearest 100 units; does not include wagon production which was 185,500. Exact model year production was 1,499,876.

Model no.	Fisher style no.	Type vehicle
1966 Biscayne		
153/154	15369	4d Sed
153/154	15311	2d Sed
153/154	15335	4d Sta Wag (2S)
1966 Bel Air		
155/156	15569	4d Sed
155/156	15511	2d Sed
155/156	15545	4d Sta Wag (3S)
155/156	15535	4d Sta Wag (2S)
1966 Impala		
163/164	16369	4d Sed
163/164	16339	4d Spt Sed
163/164	16337	2d Spt Cpe
163/164	16367	2d Conv
163/164	16345	4d Sta Wag (3S)
163/164	16335	4d Sta Wag (2S)

Model no.	Fisher style no.	Type vehicle
1967 Biscayne		
153/154	15369	4d Sed
153/154	15311	2d Sed
153/154	15335	4d Sta Wag (2S)
1967 Bel Air		
155/156	15569	4d Sed
155/156	15511	2d Sed
155/156	15545	4d Sta Wag (3S)
1967 Impala		
163/164	16369	4d Sed
163/164	16339	4d Spt Sed
163/164	16337	2d Spt Cpe
163/164	16367	2d Conv
163/164	16345	4d Sta Wag (3S)
163/164	16335	4d Sta Wag (2S)
1967 Impala SS		
167/168	16737	2d Spt Cpe
167/168	16767	2d Conv

Model no.	Fisher style no.	Type vehicle
1967 Caprice		
166	16639	4d Spt Sed
166	16647	2d Spt Cpe
166	16645	4d Sta Wag
166	16635	4d Sta Wag

Totals

Biscayne six	54,200
Biscayne V-8	38,600
Bel Air six	41,500
Bel Air V-8	195,300
Impala six	18,800
Impala V-8	556,800
Impala SS six	400
Impala SS V-8	73,600
Caprice	124,500

Source: Standard Catalog of American Cars 1946-1975.

Note: Fisher style no. shown for 6-cyl; production includes 6-cyl and V-8. Caprice was V-8-only model; for Impala SS, only 400 sixes built. Production totals rounded off to nearest 100 units; does not include wagon production which was 155,100. Exact model year production was 1,141,822.

Model no.	Fisher style no.	Type vehicle
1968 Biscayne		
153/154	15369	4d Sed
153/154	15311	2d Sed
153/154	15335	4d Sta Wag (2S)
1968 Bel Air		
155/156	15569	4d Sed
155/156	15511	2d Sed
155/156	15545	4d Sta Wag (3S)
155/156	15535	4d Sta Wag (2S)
1968 Impala		
163/164	16369	4d Sed
163/164	16339	4d Spt Sed
163/164	16387	2d Spt Cpe
164	16467	2d Conv
164	16447	2d Cus Cpe
164	16445	4d Sta Wag (3S)
164	16435	4d Sta Wag (2S)
1968 Caprice		
166	16639	4d Spt Sed
166	16647	2d Spt Cpe
166	16645	4d Sta Wag (3S)
166	16635	4d Sta Wag (2S)

Totals

Biscayne six	44,500
Biscayne V-8	37,600
Bel Air six	28,800
Bel Air V-8	123,400
Impala six	11,400
Impala V-8	699,500
Caprice	115,500

Source: Standard Catalog of American Cars 1946-1975.

Note: Fisher style no. shown for 6-cyl, except V-8-only models. Caprice and Impala Custom Coupe, convertible and wagon were V-8-only models. Production includes 6-cyl and V-8. Production totals rounded off to nearest 100 units; does not include wagon production which was 175,600. Exact model year production was 1,236,405.

Model no.	Fisher style no.	Type vehicle
1969 Biscayne		
153/154	15369	4d Sed
153/154	15311	2d Sed
153/154	15336	4d Sta Wag (2S)
1969 Bel Air		
155/156	15569	4d Sed
155/156	15511	2d Sed
156	15646	4d Sta Wag
156	15636	4d Sta Wag
1969 Impala		
163/164	16369	4d Sed
163/164	16339	4d Spt Sed
163/164	16337	2d Spt Cpe
164	16447	2d Formal Cpe
164	16667	2d Conv
164	16646	4d Sta Wag
164	16636	4d Sta Wag
1969 Caprice		
166	16639	4d Spt Sed
166	16647	2d Formal Cpe
166	16646	4d Sta Wag (3S)
166	16636	4d Sta Wag

Totals

Biscayne six	27,400
Biscayne V-8	41,300
Bel Air six	17,000
Bel Air V-8	139,700
Impala six	8,700
Impala V-8	768,300
Caprice	166,900

continued

Source: Standard Catalog of American Cars 1946-1975.
Note: Fisher style no. shown for 6-cyl, except V-8-only models. Bel Air station wagons, Impala Formal Coupe, convertible, station wagon and Caprice were V-8 only. Production for 6-cyl and V-8. Production totals rounded off to nearest 100 units; does not include wagon production which was 59,300. Impala SS-427 production was 2,455 units. Exact model year production was 1,109,013.

Model no.	Fisher style no.	Type vehicle
1970 Biscayne/Brookwood		
153/154	69	4d Sed
154	36	4d Sta Wag (2S)
1970 Bel Air/Townsman		
155/156	69	4d Sed
156	46	4d Sta Wag (3S)
156	36	4d Sta Wag (2S)
1970 Impala/Kingswood		
163/164	69	4d Sed
163/164	37	2d Spt Cpe
164	39	4d Spt Sed
164	47	2d Cus Cpe
164	67	2d Conv
164	46	4d Sta Wag (3S)
164	36	4d Sta Wag (2S)

Model no.	Fisher style no.	Type vehicle
1970 Caprice/Kingswood Estate		
166	39	4d Spt Sed
166	47	2d Spt Cpe
166	46	4d Sta Wag (3S)
166	36	4d Sta Wag (2S)
Totals		
Biscayne six		12,300
Biscayne V-8		23,100
Bel Air six		9,000
Bel Air V-8		66,800
Impala six		6,500
Impala V-8		612,800
Caprice		92,000

Source: Standard Catalog of American Cars 1946-1975.
Note: Six-cylinder (when offered) model numbers appear to left of column one slash.

Chapter 8

1971-72 Impala and Caprice

★★★★	1971-72 Impala convertible (with 454)
★★★	1971-72 Caprice Custom and Sport Coupe (with 454)
★★★	1971-72 Impala convertible
★★	1971-72 Caprice Custom and Sport Coupe
★★	1971-72 Impala Custom and Sport Coupe (with 454)
★	1971-72 Impala Custom and Sport Coupe
★	1971-72 Caprice Sport Sedan (with 454)
★	1971-72 Caprice Kingswood Estate wagon (with 454)

A new front with sculptured hood, custom-styled grille and recessed headlamps was used on 1971 Chevrolets. New for that year were an improved Advanced Full Coil suspension, power disc/drum brakes, open construction rocker panels, double panel roof construction, thinner windshield pillars and flush door handles. Sealed side terminal batteries were also introduced. Other innovations were molded door panels and a power ventilation system with deck lid louvers. The 1972 models grew again and received a facelift. Power brakes and steering and auto-

This 1971 Caprice (Sport) Sedan featured a new power ventilation system, new suspension and longer wheelbase. Disc/drum brakes were standard for second year.

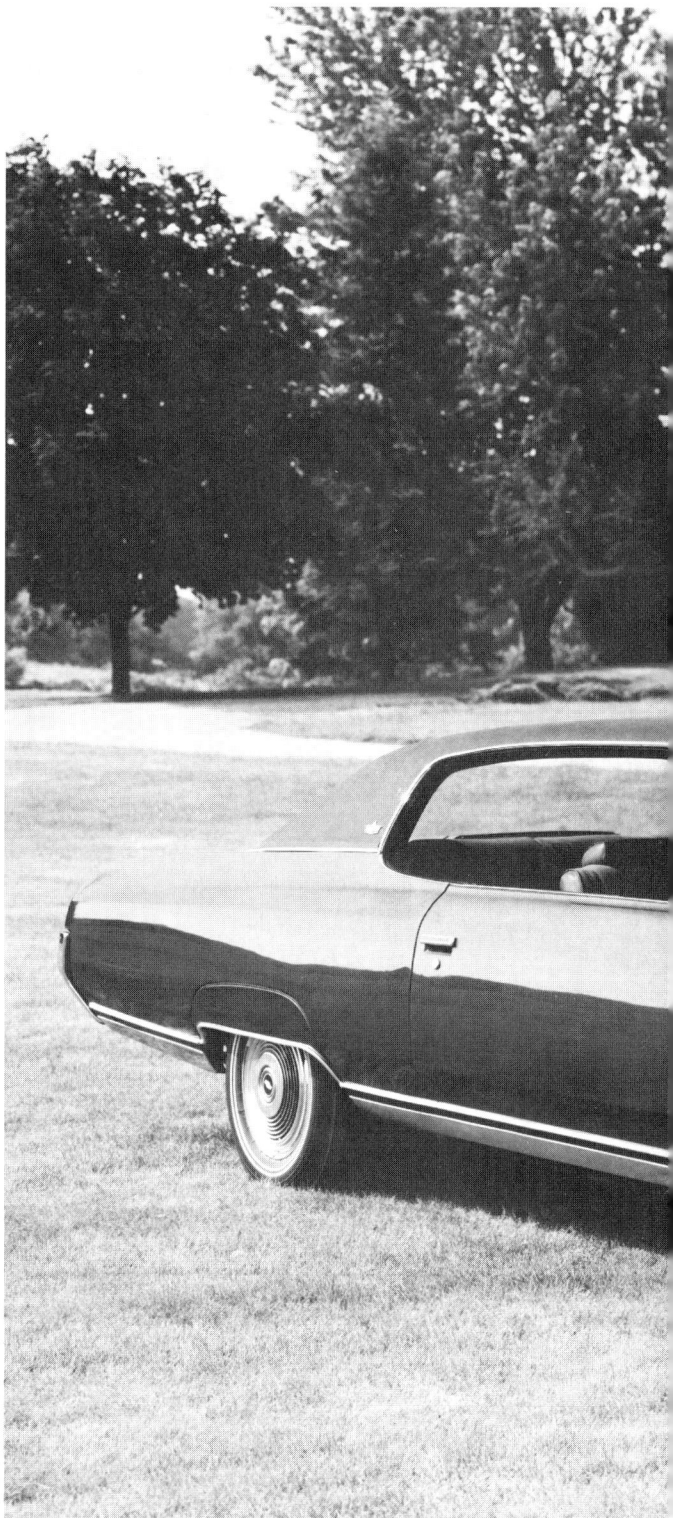

Unique egg-crate grille was used on 1971
Caprices like this hardtop coupe. Trim included
crests on grille and sail panels and V-8 engine
call-out behind front wheel. Fender skirts were
standard.

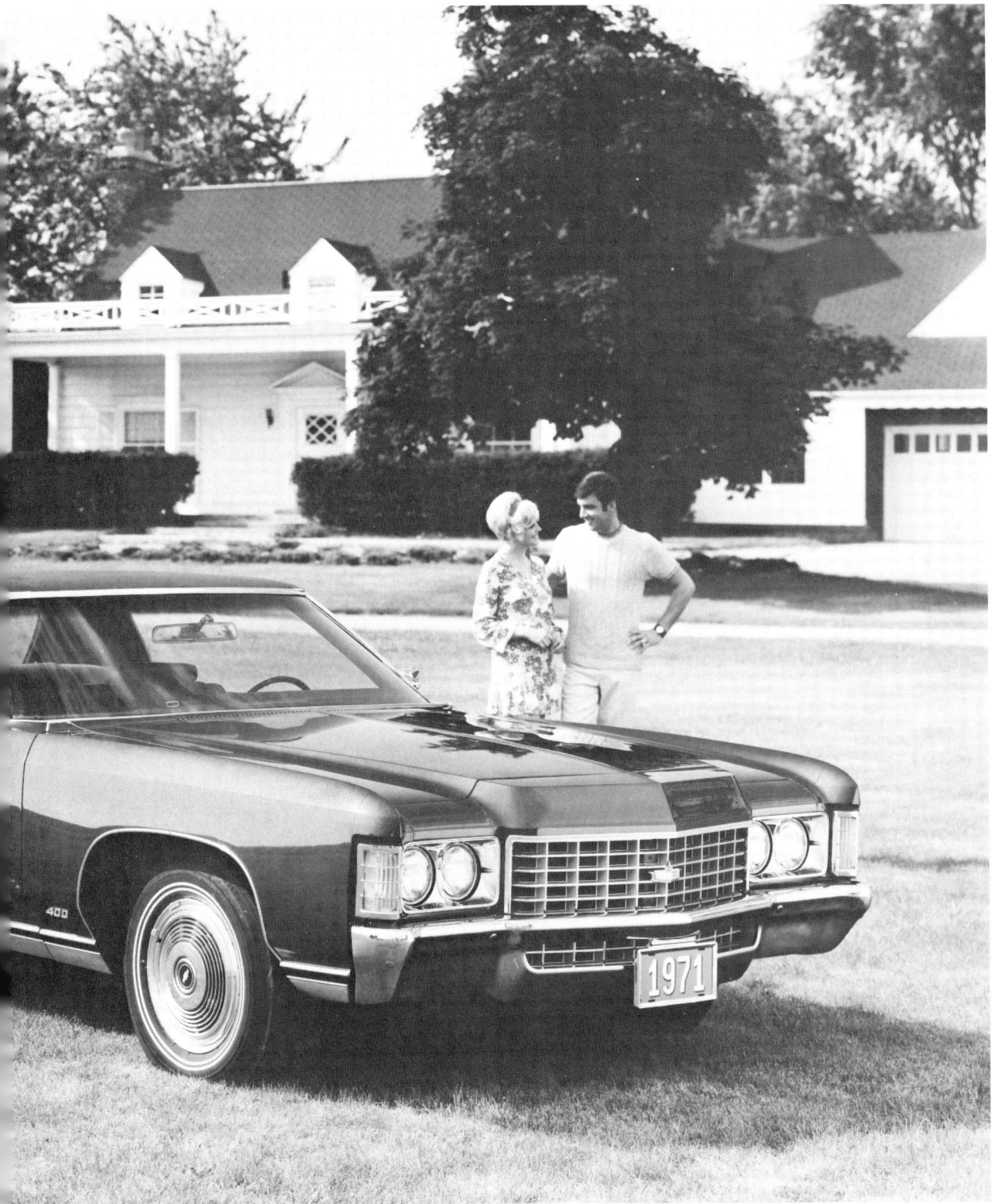

matic transmission became standard equipment.

The serial numbering for 1971 was a continuation of the previous system, but was changed in 1972. The first symbol remained a numeral 1 for Chevrolet, followed by a letter indicating car line: K=Biscayne; L=Bel Air; M=Impala; and N=Caprice. The third and fourth symbols indicated body style. The fifth symbol indicated engine; sixth represented model year; and seventh indicated assembly plant. The last six digits were the unit production number.

The 1971 and 1972 full-size Chevrolets look similar, with egg-crate grilles, dual horizontal headlamps and vertical parking lamps in the front fender tips characterizing 1971 models. The louvered rear deck lid proved prone to water leaks and was dropped for 1972. Also, the 1972 grilles are slimmer with a finer texture. Parking lamps were smaller vertical slashes in the front fender tips and a crest was placed on the hood lip above the grille. The 1972 bodyside feature-line was placed much lower, and Caprices had new bumper impact strips.

Standard equipment for Biscaynes included a windshield antenna; Astro-Ventilation; concealed wipers; side-guard door beams; heater/defroster; cigar lighter; locking glovebox; center dome light; armrests; inside hood release; left outside rearview (OSRV) mirror; and cloth trim. Bel Airs also had a glovebox light and cloth and vinyl upholstery. Impalas added a trunk light; vinyl-trimmed pattern cloth upholstery; wood-grained dash; deluxe steering wheel (with cushioned center and forward mounted gear and linkage); and foam front seat cushions. Caprices in 1971 had a grille with deeper recessed openings and a bow-tie badge in its center. In 1972, the Impala grille had horizontal fins, while the Caprice stayed with an egg-crate style. Caprice standard equipment also included ashtray and courtesy lamps; electric clock; fender skirts; distinctive cloth

Frontal styling had new, squared-off look for 1972. Headlamps were individualized; Chevy script appeared on left side of grille. Parking lamps moved into bumper. Side-markers in front were of a new twin segment design.

Rear view of 1972 Caprice Sedan (actually a Sport Sedan or four-door hardtop) shows year's lower, wider body moldings with color-coordinated vinyl inserts. Wet-look vinyl roofs in choice of five colors were new.

and vinyl seat trim; color-keyed wheel covers; G78x15 tires; and a 350 ci 225 hp V-8 (also standard in Impala sport models). The Impala convertibles also featured courtesy lamps, carpeted lower door panels and all-vinyl upholstery.

Chevy offered fifteen Magic-Mirror acrylic lacquer finishes in 1971, of which twelve were new that season. There were six two-tone combinations available, too. The color count was the same for 1972, but only five of the same colors were carried over.

For 1972, the 250 ci 110 nhp engine was base equipment in all big Chevys available with a six, and the 350 ci 165 nhp engine was standard V-8 in most models. However, Caprices and all station wagons used the 400 ci 170 nhp V-8 as base equipment. Other options included a 350 ci 200 nhp four-barrel V-8 with single exhausts; a 350 ci 255 nhp four-barrel V-8 with dual exhausts; a 402 ci 210 nhp four-barrel V-8; and a 454 ci 270 nhp four-barrel V-8. Transmission attachments were comparable to those of 1971.

The discontinuation of the full-size Super Sport made it obvious that the high-performance big-car era had come to an end. In February 1972, *Motor Trend* did a comparison test between a Ford LTD with a 400 ci V-8 and a Caprice with Chevy's 400 ci 170 nhp V-8 and Turbo Hydramatic transmission. The magazine noted that Chevy's shorter-stroke engine should have been slightly better performing, but found that differences in automatic transmission design made the Ford slightly faster. The Caprice took 11.3 seconds to move from 0-60 mph and required 18.4 seconds to cover the quarter-mile at 76 mph. The testers concluded that both of the cars were equally matched and said that a blindfolded driver would not know the difference between the two. But even a blindfolded enthusiast could tell that acceleration wasn't what it used to be a few years earlier.

Consumer magazines liked the room, ride and braking of big 1971 Chevy sedans and found them good in nearly all aspects, espe-

The 1972 Kingswood Estate wagon featured woodgrain exterior paneling. Custom wheel covers shown here were an option for all big Chevys. Wagons had unique taillamp design.

cially their nimble handling. Front seating comfort (foam-cushioned) was exceptionally well regarded. The V-8/Turbo Hydra-matic engine/transmission combination was commended for its smoothness and responsiveness.

Prospects

Good, but not perfect, full-size Chevys of these years—the kind of cars you typically see at classic auto auctions—seem to be generating spirited bidding at such sales. At 1987 auctions, there were only seven offerings and two actual sales for these cars, but the high bid or selling prices were strong.

Ownership

Incidence of repair rates for Chevys dropped off somewhat in these years. Typical owner complaints were mostly related to body problems, particularly among owners of 1971 V-8s, possibly due to a lot of water leakage through the louvers on the rear decks. The 1971 sixes also came in with an above-average number of exhaust system, cooling and steering gear repairs, but the 1972 six was just the opposite. In 1972 there were no outstanding problems with this en-

For 1972, the Turbo-Fire 400 V-8 came in 170 and 210 hp versions (170 hp only in California). It was the base engine for Caprices. Tim Streblow has the higher-output version with dual exhausts in his Caprice coupe. *Tim Streblow*

gine and the surveys rated it more reliable than comparable sixes.

Both the 1971 and 1972 V-8s went into the shop slightly more than the average for cars in their class. The 1971 had mechanical problems with the driveline and cooling system, but the 1972 had no outstanding mechanical repair needs. For that car, again it was primarily problems with bodies that dealers reported.

In his book *Chevy V-8s* (Dragonwyck Publishing), noted Chevrolet expert Terry V. Boyce mentions the 1971 Caprice Custom Coupe—a clean car with lots of options—as a model that he has seen bring $3,000 at a Florida auction. Boyce feels Impala convertibles are the best Chevys of these years to invest in. He warns they should have the 454 V-8, the fanciest factory wheel covers and a good selection of original accessories to ensure collector appeal.

Since the stock market crash in the fall of 1987, there has been a great deal of publicity about collector car investments as an alternative to stocks and bonds. This has revived a lot of interest in convertibles of the 1970s and should make the big-block, heavily op-

tioned Impala ragtops a very good, four-star investment for a while. The sporty Impala and Caprice two-door hardtops and Custom Coupes should also benefit from interest spinning off of the convertible market. Further down the line, the Caprice Sport Sedan and Kingswood Estate station wagon will probably continue to retain modest appeal to collectors.

Caprice interiors for 1972 featured rich brocade pattern cloth and vinyl upholstery. Doors had wood-like trim on upper panel, carpeted sections at bottom. *Tim Streblow*

Tim Streblow added more modern laced spoke wheel covers to his 1972 Caprice coupe. Rubber bumper impact strips were standard on Caprice, optional on other models. *Tim Streblow*

Specifications
1971-72 Chevrolet

	1971	1972
Engine	ohv six	ohv six
Displacement (ci)	250	250
Horsepower (bhp)	145	145
Wheelbase (in.)	121.5 (125 wagon)	122 (126 wagon)
Overall length (in.)	216.8 (224 wagon)	220 (226 wagon)
Tires (in.)	F78×15 (Biscayne)	F78×15 (Biscayne)

Engines
1971 Chevrolet

Engine	Carburetion	C.R.	Ghp	SAE nhp	3-spd	PG	THM
250 ci six	1V	8.5:1	145	110	std	opt	—
350 ci V-8	2V	8.5:1	245	165	std	opt	opt
400 ci V-8	2V	8.5:1	255	170	—	—	std
400 ci V-8	4V	8.5:1	300	206	—	—	std
400 ci V-8	4V	8.5:1	—	260	—	—	std
454 ci V-8	4V	8.5:1	365	285	—	—	std

Note: 250 ci six not available in Caprice or Impala Custom Coupe, Sport Sedan or convertible. The 400 ci 260 nhp V-8 option includes dual exhausts.

Auction results for 1971-72 Chevrolets

Auction company	City/state	Year/model	Condition	High bid	Sold
Suburban Motors	Tucson, AZ	'71 Caprice	3	$2,600	no
Von Reece	Ft. Worth, TX	'71 Caprice	3	3,750	no
Leake	Tulsa, OK	'71 Caprice	2	4,100	no
Kruse	Houston, TX	'71 Impala 4d HT	3	3,200	yes
Spectrum	Northridge, CA	'71 Impala conv	3	2,650	yes
Von Reece	Ft. Worth, TX	'71 Impala Custom Cpe	3	2,500	no

Source: Old Cars Auction Results, Krause Publications, Iola, Wisconsin.

Production

Model no.	Fisher style no.	Type vehicle	Production
1971 Biscayne			
153/154	69	4d Sed	22,309
— /154	35	4d Sta Wag (2S)	5,314
1971 Bel Air			
153/156	69	4d Sed	41,986
— /156	45	4d Sta Wag (3S)	6,870
— /156	35	4d Sta Wag (2S)	12,951
1971 Impala			
163/164	69	4d Sed	136,940
163/164	57	2d Spt Cpe	53,891
— /164	39	4d Spt Sed	140,300
— /164	47	2d Cus Cpe	139,437
— /164	67	2d Conv	4,567
— /164	45	4d Sta Wag (3S)	32,311
— /164	35	4d Sta Wag (2S)	26,638
1971 Caprice			
166	39	4d Spt Sed	64,093
166	47	2d Cus Cpe	46,404
166	45	4d Sta Wag (3S)	19,010
166	35	4d Sta Wag (2S)	11,913

Note: First column shows 6-cyl (when offered)/V-8 model numbers; Caprice was V-8 only. Biscayne, Bel Air and Impala sedan and Impala Sport Coupe came with sixes.

Model no.	Fisher style no.	Type vehicle	Production
1972 Biscayne			
1K	69	4d Sed	20,538
1K	35	4d Sta Wag (2S)	8,150
1972 Bel Air			
1L	69	4d Sed	41,888
1L	45	4d Sta Wag (3S)	8,667
1L	35	4d Sta Wag (2S)	16,482
1972 Impala			
1M	69	4d Sed	184,596
1M	57	2d Spt Cpe	52,692
1M	39	4d Spt Sed	170,304
1M	47	2d Cus Cpe	183,493
1M	67	2d Conv	6,456
1M	45	4d Sta Wag (3S)	40,248
1M	35	4d Sta Wag (2S)	43,152
1972 Caprice			
1N	69	4d Sed	34,174
1N	47	2d Cus Cpe	65,513
1N	45	4d Sta Wag (3S)	34,723
1N	35	4d Sta Wag (2S)	20,281
1N	39	4d Spt Sed	78,768

Note: First column shows new division/series code; Biscayne, Bel Air and Impala sedan and Impala Sport Coupe available with 6-cyl.

Chapter 9

1964-65 Chevelle and Malibu

★★★★★	1965 Chevelle SS-396 (Z-16 option)
★★★★	1964-65 Chevelle Malibu SS convertible (with 327)
★★★	1964-65 Chevelle Malibu SS convertible
★★★	1964-65 Chevelle Malibu SS Sport Coupe (with 327)
★★★	1964-65 Chevelle Malibu convertible (with 327)
★★	1964-65 Chevelle Malibu SS Sport Coupe
★★	1964-65 Chevelle Malibu convertible
★★	1964 Chevelle Malibu two-door station wagon
★★	1964-65 Chevelle Malibu Sport Sedan (with 327)
★	1964-65 Chevelle 300 two-door station wagon
★	1965 Chevelle 300 Deluxe two-door sedan (with 327)

In terms of size, the first Chevelle fit between the big Chevys and Chevy IIs. It appealed to baby boomers who had worn out or outgrown their 1955-57 Chevys—young enthusiasts who wanted a new car the same basic size and shape of a classic Chevy. Chevelles had clean, boxy styling with a hint of sculpturing, and introduced curved-glass side windows. Engineering was conventional. The chassis was a perimeter frame supported by coil springs at all four corners. Front suspension was via unequal A-arms with an anti-sway bar standard.

The 1964 Malibu had a full-length strip of brightmetal along the beltline and Malibu rear fender script. The badge on the front fender indicates a V-8 engine. The 1965 models used the same body with a different grille and tail-lamp treatment.

A choice of six-cylinder and small-block V-8 powerplants was offered initially, along with a long list of interior convenience and dress-up accessories. Performance market extras like bucket seats, floorshifts and mag-style wheel covers were optional. After December 1984, a pair of optional 327 ci V-8s was added.

Serial numbering followed the Chevrolet system outlined for full-sized cars. The second through fifth symbols indicated series and body style. In 1964, the series codes were: 53=Chevelle 300 six; 54=Chevelle 300 V-8; 55=Chevelle Malibu six; 56=Chevelle Malibu V-8; 57=Chevelle Malibu SS six; and 58=Chevelle Malibu SS V-8. In 1965, the codes were changed as follows: 31=Chevelle 300 six; 32=Chevelle 300 V-8; 33=Chevelle 300 Deluxe six; 34=Chevelle 300 Deluxe V-8; 35=Chevelle Malibu six; 36=Chevelle Malibu V-8; 37=Chevelle Malibu SS six; and 38=Chevelle Malibu SS V-8.

Chevelles had a crosshatch pattern grille in 1964. Base 300s had plain bodysides, Malibus had full-length mid-bodyside moldings and Malibu SS models had plain bodysides with upper beltline moldings, SS emblems and spinner wheel covers. The 1965 grille had a more horizontal look with a bright bar running across the center. There was a new 300 Deluxe series with rocker panel moldings and rear cove outline trim. Malibu again had a mid-bodyside molding and taillight-to-taillight rear trim moldings. However, the Malibu SS models were plain-sided, with rocker panel brightwork and windsplits ahead of the rear wheel openings. Taillights shrunk in size the second year.

Standard on 300s was pattern cloth and vinyl trims (all-vinyl wagons), vinyl floor mats, heater/defroster, front foam cushions, electric wipers, front seatbelts (1965) and 6.95x14 blackwall tires. Deluxe 300s also had plusher upholstery with vinyl door panels, a horn-ring-type dual-spoke steering wheel and padded armrests. Malibu added color accent body moldings, back-up lamps, luxury cloth and vinyl upholstery, deep-twist carpeting, foam rear seat, electric clock, glovebox light and dashboard face

panel. Super Sports had wider rocker moldings, front bucket seats, center console, all-vinyl seats and full instrumentation.

In addition to the base six, 1964 Chevelles offered five other engines. The total was increased to seven by the end of 1965.

With peppy V-8s under the hood, the Chevelle had greater performance potential. This was recognized by writer Tom McCahill in *Mechanix Illustrated:* "I am happy to report (the Chevelle) is a top road car. With the right power options and a little tuning, the Chevelle could be a bomb," McCahill said. Initially, the hot engine was Chevy's 283 ci V-8 with a four-barrel carburetor and dual exhausts, but release of the 327 ci engine came quickly.

Among the 327s available in 1964, the more desirable (then and today) was the L-74 version. The hotter L-79, derived from a 365 hp Corvette powerplant, was added in 1965, along with softer springs, modestly updated styling, interior detail changes (such as a new gauge cluster) and extra sound insulation in Malibu. Then, on Feb. 15, 1965, the all-new Turbo-Jet 396 V-8 was released as part of a Z-16 model option.

This was an integrated regular production option (RPO), meaning other specific features came in the package. They included dual exhausts and chrome engine accents; four-speed manual transmission; special suspension and shocks; 160 mph speedometer; AM/FM stereo multiplex radio; Malibu SS front fender emblems; special rear cove panel; 396 ci Turbo-Jet front fender and dash call-outs; fifteen-inch-wide simulated mag wheel covers and Firestone 7.75x14 goldline tires. All 396s were assembled at Chevy's Kansas City plant.

At a press party introducing the car, Tom McCahill entered the cockpit of a 396-SS and registered a 0-60 mph run in around six seconds. Zero-to-100 mph took only ten seconds longer and McCahill concluded that the 396-SS Chevelle reminded him of a Jaguar XKE. Other test drivers also found the car considerably faster than earlier Chevelles.

During 1965, the Malibu 396-SS was a rare car because of limited engine production capacity; only 201 were built. Most were sent to dealers as demonstrators, few went directly to the public.

The 396-SS engine featured a hydraulic camshaft. It was derived from the 409 ci 1963 NASCAR Daytona Mystery Engine, which had looked quite impressive on race-tracks before GM's high-performance ban. It featured Chevy's famous Mark IV porcupine cylinder heads.

Ownership

While the high-performance-optioned Chevelle was a great car for street enthusiasts, the man-in-the-street found the base-equipped mid-size Chevy a bit less appealing. Both the six-cylinder and V-8 powered editions made *Consumer Reports'* list of undesirable models. This appraisal was based on the average amount of repairs required.

Buyer surveys pinpointed body rattles as a major source of trips to the repair shop. The 1964 sixes also had far more than normal carburetor and transmission service requirements. The V-8s of the same year needed far more than average amount of electrical system work. Improvements were made to both series for 1965, but didn't eliminate rattles. In addition, V-8 owners found rust more of a problem that year. Other repair needs were about average for US mid-size cars, but the overall durability seemed low for early Chevelles.

Prospects

In the collector market, early Chevelles generate less excitement than later models. Knowledgeable enthusiasts feel that newer editions—1970, 1969, 1967, 1966, 1968, 1971 and 1972 in that order—have more of a supercar image. The 396 powered 1965s are a big exception, however. These are so rare that they warrant up to $20,000.

There's not a lot of market data on Chevelles in general, though. Only six 1964s and seven 1965s made the auction circuit last year, registering six actual sales. High-end prices were mostly in the $5,500 range for Malibu SS convertibles; however, one 1965 ragtop in decent condition changed hands at $1,350.

As you can see, there is some room to buy low, sell high on a short-term investment basis—but not much. And you shouldn't expect miracles when it comes to a long-term investment. The early Chevelles just aren't booming like a Pontiac GTO of the same era, except for the Z-16. There's a reason for this. The 1964 GTO quickly took on an identity totally separate from the mid-size LeMans it was based on. Chevelles—even Malibus—didn't quite have the same type of distinctiveness, until 1966. During that year, the performance model, renamed the SS-396, gained more of a unique identity. Although the production of this model climbed, its desirability level increased. As is true with many Chevrolet products, rarity counted less than popularity when it came to collectibility. So, even though the later SS-396s are more readily available, they also seem to be the better investment cars today. You can still find them at bargain prices on the streets and net a nice profit, but the same can't be said of the high-dollar 1965 Z-16, which is rare to find and expensive to purchase.

Other affordable early Chevelles that are worth a second look from collectors include just about any convertible or Sport Coupe with V-8 power. The two-door station wagons also have a little extra collector appeal. The same could be said of the four-door hardtop (Sport Sedan) or the lightweight 1965 Deluxe 300 two-door sedan, when equipped with a 327 ci V-8. When it comes to big engines, though, it's a good idea to check serial numbers and documentation very carefully. Make sure that the engine in the car is the one that went in at the factory.

Specifications
1964-65 Chevelle/Malibu

	1964	1965
Engine	ohv six	ohv six
Displacement (ci)	194.4	194.4
Horsepower (bhp)	120	120
Wheelbase (in.)	115	115
Overall length (in.)	193.9	196.6
Tires (in.)	6.50×14	6.95×14

Note: *All basic specifications apply to lowest-priced four-door sedan.*

Engines
1964-65 Chevelle

Code	Type	Ci	Carburetion	C.R.	Bore×stroke	Bhp	Price
1964							
L-26	I-6	230	1V	8.5:1	3.875×3.25	140	$43
—	V-8	283	2V	9.25:1	3.88×3.00	195	109
L-77	V-8	283	4V	9.25:1	3.88×3.00	220	54
L-30	V-8	327	4V	10.5:1	4.00×3.25	250	95
L-74	V-8	327	4V	10.5:1	4.00×3.25	300	138
1965							
L-26	I-6	230	1V	8.5:1	3.875×3.25	140	26
—	V-8	283	2V	9.25:1	3.88×3.00	195	109
L-77	V-8	283	4V	10.5:1	3.88×3.00	220	54
L-30	V-8	327	4V	10.5:1	4.00×3.25	250	93
L-79	V-8	327	4V	11.0:1	4.00×3.25	350	198
Z-16	V-8	396	4V	10.25:1	4.09×3.76	375	—

Performance
Early Chevelle

Year/model	Ci/Bhp	0-60 mph	¼ mile
1964 Malibu SS Sport Coupe	283/195	9.7 sec	17.4 sec
1965 Malibu SS Sport Coupe	283/220	9.7	17.5
1965 Malibu 396-SS Sport Coupe	396/375	6.5	14.9

Production

Model no. 6-cyl	Model no. V-8	Type vehicle
1964 Chevelle 300		
5369	5469	4d Sed
5311	5411	2d Sed
5335	5435	4d Sta Wag
5315	5415	2d Sta Wag
1964 Chevelle Malibu		
5569	5669	4d Sed
5537	5637	2d Spt Cpe
5567	5667	2d Conv
5545	5645	4d Sta Wag
5535	5635	4d Sta Wag

1964 Chevelle Malibu SS

5737	5837	2d Spt Cpe
5767	5867	2d Conv

Totals

Spt Cpe	134,670
4d Sed	113,816
4d Sta Wag	41,374
Conv	23,158
2d Sed	22,588
2d Sta Wag	2,710

Source: Jerry Heasley.

Note: Ward's Automotive Yearbook *listed total production at 338,346. The difference of thirty cars cannot be explained.*

Model no. 6-cyl	Model no. V-8	Type vehicle
1965 Chevelle 300		
13169	13269	4d Sed
13111	13211	2d Sed
13115	13215	2d Sta Wag
1965 Chevelle Deluxe 300		
13369	13469	4d Sed
13311	13411	2d Sed
13335	13435	4d Sta Wag
1965 Chevelle Malibu		
13569	13669	4d Sed
13537	13637	2d Spt Cpe
13567	13667	2d Conv
13535	13635	4d Sta Wag

Model no. 6-cyl	Model no. V-8	Type vehicle
1965 Chevelle Malibu SS		
13737	13837	2d Spt Cpe
13767	13867	2d Conv
Totals		
Spt Cpe		152,650
4d Sed		108,278
4d Sta Wag		35,938
2d Sed		25,595
Conv		19,765
2d Sta Wag		1,668

Source: Jerry Heasley.

Chapter 10

1966-67 Chevelle and Malibu

★★★★★	1966-67 Chevelle Malibu SS-396 convertible/Sport Coupe
★★★★	1966-67 Chevelle Malibu convertible (with 327)
★★★	1966-67 Chevelle Malibu Sport Coupe (with 327)
★★★	1967 Chevelle Concours Estate wagon (with 327)
★★★	1966-67 Chevelle Malibu convertible (with 283)
★★	1966-67 Chevelle Malibu Sport Coupe (with 283)
★★	1967 Chevelle Concours Estate wagon (with 283)
★★	1966-67 Chevelle Malibu convertible
★	1966-67 Chevelle Malibu Sport Coupe
★	1966-67 Chevelle Malibu Sport Sedan (V-8)
★	1966-67 Chevelle 300 Deluxe two-door sedan (with 327)

Chevelles were restyled for 1966; they looked like cigars with tips flattened on an angle. Feature-lines were much rounder and very eye-appealing. Two-door hardtops had a Flying Buttress roof treatment with sleek appearance. The SS-396 gained individuality with twin power blister hoods. Size was increased a fraction of an inch, but the cars looked much larger. Two-door wagons were discontinued for 1966. A mild facelift char-

The 1966 Chevelle SS-396 Sport Coupe had the Super Sport name spelled out on its rear fenders, a black-accented grille, simulated hood scoops and SS-396 badges on the grille and rear cove. *Chevrolet Motor Division*

A fancy four-door Concours Estate wagon with special black grille accents, woodgrain paneling, wheelhouse moldings, ribbed rocker panel moldings and a rear fender namescript was introduced in 1967. *Chevrolet Motor Division*

acterized 1967 Chevelles. New for that year were government-mandated safety equipment and a fancy Concours Estate wagon.

Serial numbering followed the 1965 system with the sixth digit changed to a numeral 6 for 1966 and 7 for 1967. Series codes were the same as in 1965. Concours wagons carried the same series coding as 1965 Super Sports: 137 for sixes and 138 for V-8s.

A crosshatched grille and dual headlamps with trim between them characterized 1966 models. The bumper had small slots with parking lamps in the outer slots; taillamps were curved horizontal type. The 1967s had a grille with more prominent horizontal members, and trim between the headlamps disappeared. The bumper had one long, horizontal slot with parking lamps in the extreme ends. Taillamps moved to the rear fender tips and could be seen from the side.

Chevelle 300s had plain bodysides, rear coves and taillamps. Deluxes added a simple mid-body side molding in 1966. In 1967 they had no side trim, but featured rocker panel moldings. The 1966 Malibu also had no side trim except rocker panel strips, but had moldings on the rear cove, plus fancier taillamps. For 1967, trim along the lower feature-line, on Malibus, replaced bright rocker panel highlights. In addition, the 1967 Malibu taillamps were segmented by a chrome strip. For both years, the SS-396 featured rocker panel trim, hood scoops, SS emblems, blackout grilles and a special rear cove treatment (aluminized in 1966; blacked out in 1967). Red-stripe tires were standard on the SS-396.

Equipment features varied by series. Basically, the 300s had low-level cloth and vinyl upholstery and rubber floor mats, while Deluxes had vinyl door panels, deluxe steering wheels and color-keyed upper instrument panels. Malibus added carpeting, black crackle (for 1966) or walnut (for 1967) instrument panel finish, bright roof rails, richer upholstery and full wheel covers. Super Sports had the features already described, plus all-vinyl upholstery, specific wheel covers and—most importantly—a 396

A new annodized aluminum grille and minor sheet metal changes were seen on 1967 Chevelles. Tom Gawrodski's Malibu Sport Coupe has the base six-cylinder engine.

ci V-8. Bucket seats were optional, however. The 1967 Concours wagons came with sixes or optional V-8s. They had SS-like ribbed gray rocker panel moldings and black-accented grilles, plus woodgrain exterior paneling.

The 1966-67 Chevelles had a number of powertrain changes. Base engines were carried over. Options were expanded from six to eight for 1966, and some old horsepower ratings were adjusted. The L-30 increased twenty-five horsepower to 275. New extras included 325 and 360 hp versions of the Turbo-Jet 396. The 325 hp version was standard in Super Sports, while the 360 hp was a street performance version with a hotter hydraulic cam. Switching from the superhot hydraulic cam featured in 1965, the 1966 L-78 had mechanical (solid) lifters and 375 hp.

By 1967, some output ratings started heading downward. The L-79 version of the 327 ci engine went from 350 to 325 hp, and the L-34 version of the 396 went from 360 to 350 hp. Both the base Turbo-Jet 396 and the L-78 were untouched. A new big six was also introduced. It had twenty additional cubic inches and fifteen more horsepower.

Although the SS-396 became more available, it was still an integrated package rather than strictly an engine option. Chassis components were specially beefed-up. The 396 ci V-8 was available only in the Malibu SS (and El Camino) models and you could not get an SS with any other engine. Although the prices of these models had climbed drastically from 1965, both the 1966s and 1967s retailed for less than $2,800 in "standard" form, which included a heavy-duty three-speed manual transmission with floor shifter.

Adding the L-34 engine took an additional $105, while the L-78 price tag was $237 extra. Despite its 375 hp rating, enthusiasts believe that the latter engine developed over 400 hp. The L-78 is not listed in all Chevelle sales literature, but remained available through 1969. Some sources indicate that only 100 of the L-78s were sold in 1966. This appears to be incorrect, however. It's now believed that as many as 10,000 cars may have carried the option.

Sexy, recessed back window treatment was used on 1966 and 1967 Chevelle Sport Coupes. It's illustrated here by Tom Gawrodski's 1967 Malibu six. Malibus featured vinyl interior trim and woodgrained dashboard accents.

Disc brakes were introduced as part of a factory option package in 1967. This option also included Argent Silver Rally-styled wheels. Although the disc brakes were problem prone, collectors consider cars so-equipped to be more desirable because of these rare wheels.

Among other desirable 1966-67 Chevelle options are four-speed manual transmission ($184 for Chevelles; $105 for SS-396s); Strato bucket seats ($111); All-Weather air conditioning ($311); Special Instrumentation ($79); push-button AM/FM radio ($134); mag-style wheel covers ($53); tachometer ($47); and a vinyl top ($74). These are average prices and varied slightly depending on model year and mix of other options. Basically, the more options a car has, the better its investment picture becomes.

Ownership

Frequent trips to Chevrolet dealer service departments remained a part of the Chevelle's service history for 1966 and 1967 models. Both sixes and V-8s were again rated undesirable by *Consumer Reports*. Body durability and automatic transmissions were major problems. Manual gearboxes, fuel and exhaust systems and shock absorbers caused problems, too. The 1967s were slightly more reliable than the 1966s—especially in terms of their exhaust systems—but the overall service profile looked bleak in owner surveys.

Prospects

This has little influence on current collectibility though, judging by auction results. Hardtops in top shape are drawing bids as high as $9,000 today, while SS-396 convertibles in like condition have sold for as high as $13,500. High bids have also been registered for modified Chevelles, such as a 1966 Sport Coupe with a 427 ci V-8 ($16,500) and a 1967 SS-396 with custom paint ($14,000). Other bids run all over the ballpark, as low as $2,800 for a ragtop in mid-scale condition.

Recently, one veteran collector stated that an SS-396 Chevelle isn't a true muscle car because it has less than a 400 ci engine. I feel this is a misconception. First, some Chevelles with over 400 ci engines were constructed as stock car or drag-racing machines. In addition, other models (at least 500 in 1969) were specially optioned with RPO L-72—the Corvette 427 ci 425 hp engine. And, of course, the SS-454 of 1970-75 was a real powerhouse in some of those

years. However, you can bet that the SS-396's fourteen-second quarter-miles at over 100 mph make it a legitimate muscle car, regardless of its cubic inch displacement figure.

Certainly, 327 powered Chevelles (especially L-79s) are also good cars to invest in. This combination has a lot going for it when it comes to street performance, and some collectors *do* enjoy driving their cars regularly. In fact, the four-barrel, dual exhaust version of the 283 ci V-8 with 220 hp, shouldn't be overlooked either. The point is, you can invest in just about any of these Chevelles and come out in the two- to four-star rating category.

Some high-performance buffs (and magazines catering to them) insist that Sport Coupes are equally or more desirable than convertibles as muscle car investments. When the muscle car era was in its heyday, these coupes were favored by drag racers, since the convertibles were slower in the quarter-mile due to their heavier weight and less streamlined character. As a result, when the cars were new, coupes outsold ragtops by a wide margin.

Current market data suggests, however, that convertibles are now the top choice of

Malibu script decorated rear fenders on the 1967 models. New vertically segmented taillamps replaced the earlier horizontal lenses.

Rectangular back-up lamps were housed in the rear bumper. Full wheel covers were standard equipment on Malibus.

collectors. Rarity is one reason for this, but the basic appeal of top-down driving counts for a lot, too. Collectors don't usually race their cars, so lighter weight and sleeker lines aren't a factor. Enthusiasts who enjoy competing in nostalgia drag racing may like Sport Coupes best, but it seems convertibles are still king of the hill when it comes to world-record prices.

In terms of investment potential, things do not seem to be as clear-cut, however. For example, SS-396 Sport Coupes seem to be appreciating at just as fast a rate as SS-396 convertibles, when it comes to their percentage increase in value. In other words, a coupe with the 396 ci engine—selling for $6,000 today—might bring $12,000 in three to five years, while an SS-396 convertible worth $15,000 now may bring $30,000 after the same period of time has passed.

When the 396 ci high-performance engine is taken out of the picture, trim levels and body styles begin to have a bigger effect on the investment angle. For instance, a 327 powered Malibu convertible gets a four-star rating, versus three stars for a Malibu Sport Coupe with the same engine.

More affordable investments include the '67 Concours Estate wagon with a 283 or 327 ci V-8, or a six-cylinder Malibu convert-ible. Unless the top goes down, I would suggest staying away from the sixes, because they just don't excite collectors. On the other hand, a plain-Jane 300 Deluxe two-door sedan with the 327 ci engine might bring a higher price than expected. The combination of a relatively big engine in a lightweight car has appeal to enthusiasts who would enjoy blowing the doors off a fancy small-block-engined competitor at a red light. Such cars have to be in exceptionally fine condition (almost like new) to have special value to collectors; otherwise, it's a good idea to skip the "cheap" models and stick to the sportier body styles like convertibles and Sport Coupes.

Specifications
1966-67 Chevelle/Malibu

	1966	1967
Engine	ohv six	ohv six
Displacement (ci)	194	194
Horsepower (bhp)	120	120
Wheelbase (in.)	115	115
Overall length (in.)	196.6	197
Tires (in.)	6.95×14	7.35×14

Note: Base specifications apply to lowest-priced four-door sedan.

Engines
1966 Chevelle

Code	Type	Ci	Carburetion	C.R.	Bore×stroke	Bhp@rpm
L-26	I-6	230	1V	8.5:1	3.875×3.25	140@4400
—	V-8	283	2V	9.25:1	3.88×3.00	195@4800
L-77	V-8	283	4V	9.25:1	3.88×3.00	220@—
L-30	V-8	327	4V	10.0:1	4.00×3.25	275@4800
L-79	V-8	327	4V	11.0:1	4.00×3.25	350@5800
—	V-8	396	4V	10.25:1	4.09×3.76	325@4800
L-34	V-8	396	4V	10.25:1	4.09×3.76	360@5200
L-78	V-8	396	4V	10.25:1	4.09×3.76	375@5600

1967 Chevelle

Code	Type	Ci	Carburetion	C.R.	Bore×stroke	Bhp@rpm
L-22	I-6	250	1V	8.5:1	3.875×3.53	155@4200
—	V-8	283	2V	9.25:1	3.88×3.00	195@4800
L-30	V-8	327	4V	10.0:1	4.00×3.25	275@4800
L-79	V-8	327	4V	10.0:1	4.00×3.25	325@5600
—	V-8	396	4V	10.25:1	4.09×3.76	325@4800
L-34	V-8	396	4V	10.25:1	4.09×3.76	350@5200
L-78	V-8	396	4V	10.25:1	4.09×3.76	375@5600

Performance

1966-67 Chevelle	Ci/Bhp	0-60 mph	¼ mile
1966 SS-396 2d HT	396/360	7.9 sec	15.5 sec
1966 SS-396 2d HT	396/375	6.4	14.3
1967 SS-396 2d HT	396/375	6.5	14.9

Production

Model no. 6-cyl	Model no. V-8	Type vehicle
1966 Chevelle 300		
13169	13269	4d Sed
13111	13211	2d Sed
1966 Chevelle 300 Deluxe		
13369	13469	4d Sed
13311	13411	2d Sed
13335	13435	4d Sta Wag
1966 Chevelle Malibu		
13569	13669	4d Sed
13539	13639	4d Spt Sed
13517	13617	2d Spt Cpe
13567	13667	Conv
13535	13635	4d Sta Wag

Car line	6-cyl	V-8	Total
Chevelle 300	23,300	5,300	28,600
Chevelle 300 Deluxe	27,100	10,500	37,600
Chevelle Malibu	52,300	189,300	241,600
Sta Wag	8,900	23,000	31,900
SS-396	—	72,272	72,272

Model no. 6-cyl	Model no. V-8	Type vehicle
1967 Chevelle 300		
13169	13269	4d Sed
13111	13211	2d Sed
1967 Chevelle 300 Deluxe		
13369	13469	4d Sed
13311	13411	2d Sed
13335	13435	4d Sta Wag

Model no. 6-cyl	Model no. V-8	Type vehicle
1967 Chevelle Malibu		
13569	13669	4d Sed
13517	13617	2d Spt Cpe
13567	13667	Conv
13535	13635	4d Sta Wag
13539	13639	4d Spt Sed
1967 Concours Estate		
13735	13835	4d Sta Wag
1967 SS-396		
—	13817	2d Spt Cpe
—	13867	Conv

Totals

Car line	6-cyl	V-8	Total
Chevelle 300	19,900	4,800	24,700
Chevelle 300 Deluxe	19,300	7,000	26,300
Chevelle Malibu	40,600	187,200	227,800
Sta Wag	5,900	21,400	27,300
SS-396	—	63,006	63,006

Chapter 11

1968-72 Chevelle and Malibu

★★★★★	1969 Yenko 427 Chevelle (with L-72)
★★★★★	1970 Malibu SS-454 coupe and convertible (with LS-6)
★★★★	1970-72 Malibu SS-454 convertible (with LS-5)
★★★★	1971-72 Heavy-Chevy
★★★	1970-72 Malibu SS-454 coupe (with LS-5)
★★★	1968-69 Malibu SS-396 convertible
★★	1968-69 Malibu SS-396 coupe
★★	1968-69 Malibu convertible
★	1968-69 Malibu coupe
★	1968-72 Concours Estate wagon

Chevelles made from 1968-72 represent third-generation models. Bodies had an integrated C-pillar/rear deck design with fenders and quarter panels blended smoothly into soft curves. The 1968-69 models use a wrapover frontal treatment with cut-back fenderline, and the 1970-72s have a heftier, blunter appearance. The use of a longer wheelbase for four-doors was new, and tends to have less collector appeal. However, coupes and convertibles of this era are among the most collectible Chevelles.

Serial numbering follows the 1965-67 system until 1972, when the second symbol changes to a letter (B for Nomad wagons; C for Chevelles; D for Malibus; and H for Concours Estate). The fifth symbol became the engine designator and the sixth indicated model year. The seventh symbol represented the manufacturing plant and was followed by a six-digit build sequence code.

Side-marker lamps were added to front and rear fenders of 1968 Chevelles. Here the front-markers carry 327 ci V-8 engine call-out. Malibu name on front fender behind wheel identifies series. *Chevrolet Motor Division*

Interior of this 1969 Malibu convertible has standard bench seat. Performance options include floor-mounted four-speed shifter, under-dash gauge package and tachometer. Wood-trimmed steering wheel has Chevrolet signature.

Car-line names changed, as reflected in charts at the end of this book. Super Sport equipment became an option (RPO Z-25) for the first time in 1969. The Nomad name was reintroduced for base wagons in 1970. A Heavy Chevy—offering SS goodies at a special price—made its debut in 1971. A 1972 United Automobile Workers strike held up plans for major changes that season.

Model-year identification can be made by noting styling details. In 1968, front parking lamps were below headlamps. Grilles had a wire mesh appearance and narrow, slot-like taillamps were used. In 1969, prominent horizontal bars filled the grille and parking lamps were moved to a slot in the center of the front bumper; taillamps grew larger. Chevelles had the blunter front end in 1970, with horizontally split bi-level grilles and parking lamps moved back below the head-lamps. Single headlamps were new for 1971,

New taillamps for 1969 were wider and angled inward. Cove treatment on this Malibu convertible features black-out insert. Malibu name appears on rear fendersides and below Chevelle trunk script. T. Savino owns this ragtop.

Although the 1969 Malibus came in only six basic body types, a long list of options permitted buyers to build over 300 different versions of the cars. Steve Batzko's Sport Coupe shown here has performance hood with twin power bulges, black-accented grille and Rally wheels. Lower body perimeter also has extra-cost Argent Silver finish.

Circular headlamps were set into individual square housings on the front of 1969 Chevelles. Horizontal grille bar had a bow-tie emblem in its center, except on Super Sports. Malibu ragtop belongs to T. Savino.

when new bi-level parking lamps wrapped around the front body corners. The 1972 models had tri-level grilles, one-piece wrap-around front parking lamps and round in-the-bumper taillamps.

Equipment levels followed the previous building-block approach, with bottom-line models featuring minimal trim, plainer upholstery, rubber floor mats and standard steering wheels. Standard equipment lists grew to reflect both government-required safety features and upgraded industry standards. For example, by 1971, Concours Estate wagons came with hideaway headlamps, V-8s and power front disc/rear drum brakes.

Bright new colors were part of this Chevelle generation's image; a yellow car graced the cover of the 1968 sales brochure. Inside there was a red SS-396 coupe and a gold SS-396 convertible. However, other colors—commonly seen on more mundane models—were a mixture of conservative greens, blues and grays, plus white, maroon, silver and black. The later models, of the seventies, sported some even wilder choices of finish.

Burnt orange was popular with high-performance buffs, along with lime green, Sunflower yellow, Cranberry red and Placer gold.

Collectors focus most intensely on the Super Sports, whether they were merchandised as a separate car line or as a model option. The SS package was more distinctive, starting in 1968, when matte black finish was used not only on the grille and rear end panel, but also on the full lower body perimeter. Other SS ingredients were red-stripe wide-oval tires, deluxe steering wheel, special body accent stripes, special twin domed hood, SS-396 badges, vinyl upholstery and three-speed manual transmission with floor shifter. Bucket seats remained a popular extra-cost item, of course.

As in 1966 and 1967, Chevrolet down-played its top (L-78) Chevelle power option, listing only eight standard or extra-cost engines in the 1968 sales catalog. Product order forms showed the 396 ci 375 hp choice even more clearly, however, and boosted its sales to nearly 2,000 installations. Chassis

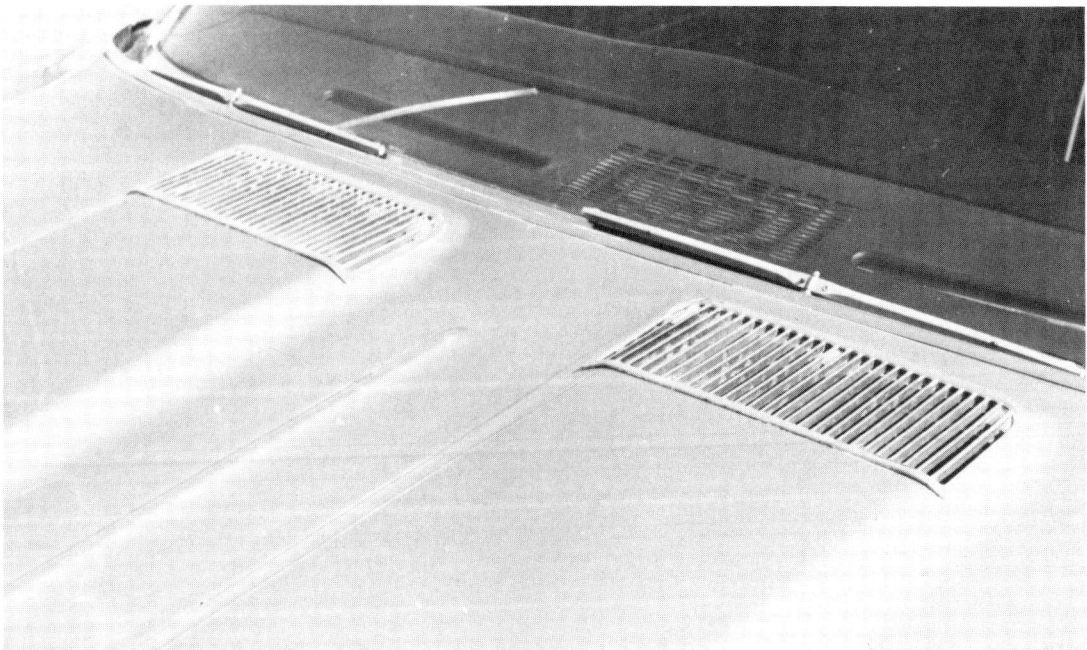

Hoods with twin power blisters were extra-cost items for both Malibu and SS-396 models of

1969. Chrome air vents were placed at the rear of blisters, near the cowl, to suck in cold air.

Chevelles with 1969 Super Sport 396 option had SS emblems in place of bow-tie in the grille, plus SS fender badges. The Turbo-Jet 396 engine was part of this model option. Hood lock pins and hood stripes were additional extras.

engineering was virtually the same as before, with coil springs all around and 9.5 in. drum brakes front and rear.

Refinements in 1969 Chevelles included ignition switches on the steering column, one-piece side glass, and upholstery and trim changes. Optional Delco front disc brakes were improved and new chrome Sport wheels were available at extra cost. Engine and transmission choices were similar, but not the same as in 1968. An extremely rare 1969 engine possibility was the special Central Office Production Order (COPO) 427 ci V-8 which was sold in the crate for owner, dealer and builder installations. A total of only 358 such engines were assembled, and only at Cheverolet's Towanda, New York, factory for use in A-bodied Chevelles. Most of these engines are believed to have been used in cars custom-converted by Don Yenko, a Chevrolet dealer who operated Yenko Sports Cars, Incorporated, in Canonsburg, Pennsylvania.

The L-78 engine option with the 396 ci 375 hp high-performance V-8 was back again for 1969 Chevelle SS-396 models. Chrome dress-up items were included in the $648 package. This engine had special lightweight aluminum cylinder heads.

Chevelles offered the former big six as standard equipment in 1970 and a new 400 ci V-8 joined the 307 and 350. This engine was part of the Turbo-Jet family, but at 300 hp it was no threat to the high-performance 396. The primary reason for making this motor available was to remain competitive with Chrysler products in the cubic inch battle. The 350 hp version of the 396 was standard for 1970 in the SS-396 models. At midyear, this engine was actually enlarged to 402 ci, although it was still called the SS-396. About the same time, in January 1970, a 454 ci was made available, too.

The release of the 454 big-block for intermediate-size cars was a reversal of the previous GM rule against engines larger than 400 ci being used in A-body cars. This, of course, was another reaction to the marketplace battle with Chrysler performance cars. The engine came in two variations. The most common was the LS-5 edition with 360 hp. The most exciting was the LS-6, which featured an 800 cfm Holley carburetor, low-profile dual plenum aluminum intake manifold, rectangular port closed-chamber cast-iron large-valve heads, solid lifter cam, forged steel crankshaft, four-bolt mains and 11.0:1 compression pistons. Some 4,500 cars were built with this option, which delivered 450 hp.

By 1971, engine choices for Chevelles dropped down to six possibilities, all with lower compression ratios, which could be linked to one of five transmissions. The SS-396 was no longer standard in cars with the Super Sport option. In addition, the SS package was made available for any V-8-powered Malibu, except those with the base 307 ci V-8.

The original SS engine returned in 1972. It was now called a 400, rather than a 396 or 402. This was still a performance engine—not to be confused with the regular 400 ci job—but its lower output rating was an indication that the muscle car era was ending. An option for the year was a slightly de-tuned version of the LS-5 for SS-454 models. It had a 270 hp SAE net rating. Another technical change was a noticeable reduction of performance axle ratios, with the hottest option having 3.31:1 gearing.

After 1970, the ingredients of the SS package included power disc/drum brakes, a black-finished grille with SS emblem, Sport suspension, special domed hood with lock pins, 15x7 inch Sport wheels, F60x15 white-letter tires and other SS identification. For 1971, as an example, the SS-350 cost $357 over base price, while the SS-454 package carried a $485 price tag.

The Heavy-Chevy was midyear 1971 package. This car featured the Super Sport hood and grille, Rally wheels, a special full-length upper bodyside decal stripe and Heavy-Chevy fender decals. The SS suspension and brakes were not included, however, and LS-5 and LS-6 engines weren't available.

Ownership

Contemporary consumer magazines found the Chevelle of these years improved. In fact, it was top-rated among two-door American intermediates and tied for first with American Motors Corporation's Matador among four-door intermediates. Comfort, roominess, handling and steering were strong points. Brakes were described as good to very good, without the disc brake option. However, mechanical woes—especially with sixes—were still typical and worse than average in 1968 and 1969.

Both sixes and V-8s had more than ordinary body and paint finish problems in 1968-69. Engine mechanical problems plagued the sixes of these years and manual gearboxes were a trouble source for V-8s. The fuel system was another sore point with six-cylinder owners. A good electrical system was one saving grace on the sixes. But over-all, both sixes and V-8s went to repair shops more often than average.

The 1970-71 Chevelles—both sixes and V-8s—were drastically improved; the best of the series built up to that point. Engine cooling and ignition problems were slightly above average in 1970 sixes, while V-8s of the same year had clutch and cooling problems that stood out. However, most other ownership aspects were good, with many requiring less-than-average attention. Overall ratings by owners were equally positive.

An entirely different service history was recorded by owners of 1972 models. V-8s of that season had major clutch and manual transmission problems, while sixes added cooling, exhaust system, fuel system and ignition woes that made the cars a likely candidate for trips to a repair shop. In all of these years, the V-8s were recommended over the sixes.

There was a recall on 1971 Chevelles to check for the possibility that the throttle-rod to throttle-rod retaining clip on the carburetor of six-cylinder models had been improperly installed at the factory. As for operating economy, the 250 ci six was the cheapest-to-drive Chevelle, providing about seventeen miles of driving per gallon of fuel; cars with the 307 ci V-8 were good for about 16 mpg in average driving. The 350 ci V-8 gave about 15 mpg; the 402 gave about 13-14 mpg and the big 454 maxed out at about 13 mpg.

Prospects

Depite their mixed new-car service rec-ords, the 1968-69 Chevelles are hot on the collector car auction circuit today. In 1987 sales, the highest price paid was $13,500 for an SS-396 hardtop in perfect condition, while a convertible in the same shape (both 1968s) brought just $8,550. Prices for 1969 SS-396 hardtops have been rung up in the $2,650 to $6,000 range, for cars in average to good shape. The bidding on 1970 Chevelles has gone a little higher, ranging from $3,400 to $6,100 for SS-396s and $5,900 for an SS-454 with cowl induction. A 1971 SS-396 in next-to-top shape was sold for $9,400, while a pair of SS-454s in like condition went for $5,800 and $7,200, respectively. However, a regular Chevelle convertible of the same vintage, but in top condition, was sold for $6,000. As for 1972 models, there were two notable transactions, both on cars in class two. The first, an SS-454, brought $4,500, while a non-SS Chevelle convertible was sold for $5,000.

Chevelle line offered both SS-396 and SS-454 model options in 1970. This is an SS-454 Sport Coupe with the special cowl induction hood, which now had a single large power blister. When this hood was ordered, sport stripes and hood lock pins were included.

Bob Schultz is the owner of this 1970 Malibu 350 convertible. It has the optional engine producing one horsepower per cubic inch. Sport stripes on hood were added as a separate extra.

A new three-tier grille was introduced for 1971 Chevelles. Letters on side of cowl indicate this car has the Super Sport model option. Single headlamps and parking lamps in fender tips were new.

The 1971 Super Sports had large SS initials in the center of the rear bumper. This model option had a $357 base price, but other extra-cost equipment was mandatory when an SS-454 was ordered. Large round in-the-bumper taillights were a well-known trademark of the Chevy A-bodies in this period.

Though hard to see in the earlier photos of this same car, the SS-454 had the engine displacement called out below the model initials on the side of the cowl. When the cowl induction hood was ordered, Sport stripes and hood lock pins were included.

The 1972 Chevelles looked very similar to the 1971s. This is the Malibu Sport Coupe in basic form with extra-cost whitewall tires. *Chevrolet Motor Division*

Experts say there are more collectors of early seventies' Chevelles than sixties' models. Of the three years (1970-72), the 1972s came in third in performance. The SS package could now be ordered on any V-8, but this 1972 Malibu does not have it.

Bruce LePane has the cowl induction hood, stripe and lock pins package on his 1972 Malibu 350 convertible. Bumper guards were optional and had rubber impact strips.

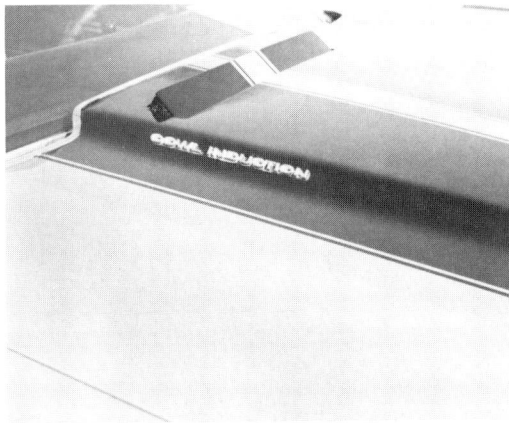

Special hood on Bruce LePane's 1972 Malibu 350 convertible has cowl induction chrome lettering on sides of power blister. Stepping on gas opened flap on scoop to shoot an extra breath of cool air into intake.

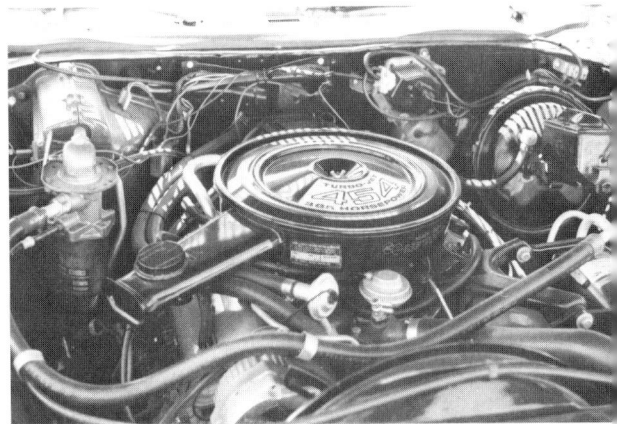

Optional Turbo-Jet 454 V-8 produced 365 gross horsepower, as indicated by its large air cleaner decal. The chrome goodies of the past were not as much in evidence on the 1970s' performance engines.

Specifications
1968-72 Chevelle/Malibu

	1968	1969	1970	1971	1972
Engine	ohv six	ohv six	ohv six	ohv six	ohv six
Displacement (ci)	230	230	250	250	250
Horsepower (bhp)	140	140	155	145	110 (SAE net)
Wheelbase (in.)	112/116	112/116	112/116	112/116	112/116
Overall length (in.)	198/202	197/201	198/202	198/202	198/202
Tires (in.)	7.35×14	7.35×14	F78×14	E78×14	E78×14

Note: Specifications apply to base level sedan. Measurements before slash are for two-door and after slash for four-door.

Engines
1968 Chevelle standard
140 hp Turbo-Thrift 230 ci six
200 hp Turbo-Fire 307 ci V-8
325 hp Turbo-Jet 396 ci V-8

1968 Chevelle options
155 hp Turbo-Thrift 250 ci six
250 hp Turbo-Fire 327 ci V-8
275 hp Turbo-Fire 327 ci V-8
325 hp Turbo-Fire 327 ci V-8
350 hp Turbo-Jet 396 ci V-8
375 hp Turbo-Jet 396 ci V-8

1969 Chevelle

Type	Ci	Bore×stroke	C.R.	Bhp	Carburetion
6-cyl	230	3.875×3.25	8.5	140	1V
6-cyl	250	3.875×3.53	8.5	155	1V
V-8	307	3.875×3.35	9.0	200	2V
V-8	350	4.001×3.48	9.0	255	4V
V-8	350	4.00×3.48	10.25	300	4V
V-8	396	4.094×3.76	10.25	325	4V
V-8	396	4.094×3.76	10.25	350	4V
V-8	396	4.094×3.76	—	375	4V

1971 Chevelle

Type and description	Ghp	Nhp
6-cyl 250 ci	145	110
V-8 307 ci	200	140
V-8 350 ci (std SS)	245	165
V-8 350 ci	270	175
V-8 400 ci	300	260
V-8 454 ci (SS-454)	365	285

Performance
1968-72 Chevelle

Year/model	Ci/Bhp	0-60 mph	¼ mile	¼ mile speed
1968 SS-396	396/375	6.6 sec	14.8 sec	98.8 mph
1969 Yenko	427/450	6.3	13.31	108.4
1969 SS-396	396/325	5.8	14.41	97.3
1970 SS-396	402/350	8.1	15.50	—
1970 SS-454	454/450	6.1	13.12	105.5
1970 SS-454	454/450	6.0	13.12	107.01

Production

Model no. 6-cyl	Model no. V-8	Type vehicle
1968 Chevelle 300		
13127	13227	2d Sed
13135	13235	4d Nomad Sta Wag
Chevelle 300 Deluxe		
13369	13469	4d Sed
13337	13437	2d Spt Cpe
13327	13427	2d Sed
13335	13435	4d Nomad Sta Wag
1968 Chevelle Malibu		
13569	13669	4d Sed
13539	13639	4d Spt Sed
13537	13637	2d Spt Cpe
13567	13667	Conv
13535	13635	4d Sta Wag
1968 Concours Estate		
13735	13835	4d Sta Wag
1968 Chevelle SS-396		
—	13837	2d Spt Cpe
—	13867	Conv

Totals

Car line	6-cyl	V-8	Total
Chevelle 300	9,700	2,900	12,600
Chevelle 300 Deluxe	25,500	17,700	43,200
Chevelle Malibu	33,100	233,200	266,300
Station wagons	10,700	34,800	45,500
SS-396	—	62,735	62,735

Model no. 6-cyl	Model no. V-8	Type vehicle
1969 Chevelle 300 Deluxe		
13369	13469	4d Sed
13337	13437	2d Spt Cpe
13327	13427	2d Sed
13135	13235	4d Nomad Sta Wag
13136	13236	4d Nomad Sta Wag
13335	13435	4d Greenbriar Wag
13336	13436	4d Greenbriar Wag
—	13446	4d Greenbriar Wag
1969 Chevelle Malibu		
13569	13669	4d Sed
13539	13639	4d Spt Sed
13537	13637	2d Spt Cpe
13567	13667	Conv
—	13646	4d Concours Wag
—	13636	4d Concours Wag

Totals

Car line	6-cyl	V-8	Total
Chevelle 300 Deluxe	11,000	31,000	42,000
Sta Wag (all)	7,400	38,500	45,900
Chevelle Malibu	23,500	343,600	367,100

Model no. 6-cyl	Model no. V-8	Type vehicle
1970 Chevelle/Nomad Wagon		
13136	13236	4d Sta Wag
1970 Chevelle Deluxe/Greenbriar Wagon		
13369	13469	4d Sed
13337	13437	2d Spt Cpe
13336	13436	4d Sta Wag (2S)
—	13446	4d Sta Wag (3S)
1970 Chevelle Malibu/Concours Wagon		
13569	13669	4d Sed
13539	13639	4d Spt Sed
13537	13637	2d Spt Cpe
13567	13667	Conv
13536	13636	4d Sta Wag (2S)
—	13646	4d Sta Wag (3S)
1970 Chevelle Concours Estate Wagon		
—	13846	4d Sta Wag (3S)
—	13836	4d Sta Wag (2S)

Totals

Car line	6-cyl	V-8	Total
Chevelle	10,700	13,200	23,900
Malibu	21,100	354,700	375,800
Sta Wag	5,600	35,000	40,600

Model no. 6-cyl	Model no. V-8	Type vehicle
1971 Chevelle/Nomad Wagon		
13136	13236	4d Sta Wag
1971 Chevelle/Greenbriar Wagon		
13369	13469	4d Sed
13337	13437	2d Spt Cpe
—	13446	4d Sta Wag (3S)
—	13436	4d Sta Wag (2S)
1971 Chevelle Malibu/Concours Wagon		
13569	13669	4d Sed
13537	13637	2d Spt Cpe
—	13639	4d Spt Sed
—	13667	Conv
—	13646	4d Sta Wag (3S)
—	13636	4d Sta Wag (2S)
1971 Chevelle Concours Estate Wagon		
—	13846	4d Sta Wag (3S)
—	13836	4d Sta Wag (2S)

Note: *Approximately 80,000 cars listed had the SS option; 19,292 were SS-454s.*

Engine type	Model no.	Type vehicle	Production
1972 Chevelle/Nomad Wagon			
6-cyl	1B36	4d Sta Wag	2,956
V-8	1B36	4d Sta Wag	7,768
1972 Chevelle Deluxe/Greenbriar Station Wagon			
6-cyl	1C69	4d Sed	6,764
V-8	1C69	4d Sed	12,881
6-cyl	1C37	2d Spt Cpe	6,993
V-8	1C37	2d Spt Cpe	22,714
V-8	1C46	4d Sta Wag (3S)	2,370
V-8	1C36	4d Sta Wag (2S)	6,975
1972 Chevelle Malibu/Concours Wagon			
6-cyl	1D69	4d Sed	3,562
V-8	1D69	4d Sed	45,013
V-8	1D39	4d Spt Sed	24,192
6-cyl	1D37	2d Spt Cpe	4,790
V-8	1D37	2d Spt Cpe	207,598
V-8	1D67	Conv	4,853
V-8	1D46	4d Sta Wag (3S)	6,560
V-8	1D36	4d Sta Wag (2S)	17,698
1972 Chevelle Concours Estate Wagon			
V-8	1H46	4d Sta Wag (3S)	4,407
V-8	1H36	4d Sta Wag (2S)	5,331

Note: A total of 24,946 cars listed had the SS option; 3,000 were SS-454s.

Chapter 12

1960-64 Corvair

★★★★★	1962-64 Monza Spyder convertible
★★★★	1962-64 Monza Spyder coupe
★★★★	1962-64 Monza convertible
★★★	1960-64 Monza coupe
★★★	1962 Monza station wagon
★★	1961-64 Monza sedan
★★	1961-62 Lakewood station wagon
★★	1960-63 Corvair 700 coupe
★	1960-64 Corvair 500 coupe
★	1961 Lakewood 500 station wagon

The Corvair has been called perhaps the most significant automobile of the postwar era. This thoroughly unconventional compact Chevy featured a rear-mounted air-cooled aluminum pancake six-cylinder engine, fully independent suspension, rear-mounted transaxle, and unitized body and frame construction. It was compact in size, but had a large impact on the American auto industry.

Corvairs were produced for ten years and fall neatly into two generations: 1960-64 and 1965-69. The first-generation models have styling characterized by a high, crisp beltline and flat, shelf-like upper body contours. These cars were introduced on Oct. 2, 1959, with a sole four-door sedan available. A coupe was a running addition to the line followed by wagons and convertibles, not to mention a line of van-like trucks which fall beyond the scope of this book.

Corvairs had a sports car image and played a popular role as a small, four-place American sports model until the Ford Mustang came along. Ford's pony car and a book by consumer advocate Ralph Nader, which criticized the safety of the Corvair's handling, led to the little Chevy's sales decline and ultimate demise.

A vehicle numbering system similar to that used on other Chevys was used for Corvair identification. Through 1964, there were twelve numbers stamped on a plate on the left-hand door pillar. The first symbol was the last digit of the model year. Next

came the model number, as shown in charts at the end of this chapter. This was followed by a symbol indicating the assembly plant, plus a six-digit build sequence number that began with 100001 at each factory.

At first, the Corvair came only in standard Corvair 500 trim and Deluxe 700 trim. Deluxes had two sun visors, chrome exterior moldings, front armrest, cigarette lighter, upgraded upholstery, color-keyed floor mats, dual horns and automatic dome lamp switch.

The Monza 900 coupe was added in February 1960. It had chrome-trimmed bucket seats, rocker sill moldings, special wheel covers, all-vinyl upholstery, chrome-trimmed rear air vents, a folding rear seat and a glovebox light.

In 1961, the Monza sedan was introduced and the next year a wagon and a convertible were added. Along with the convertible came a new Monza Spyder model option, with a coupe and convertible featuring a turbocharged 150 hp version of the same engine, plus special trim.

The Corvair station wagon was dropped from all lines in 1963. For 1964, Chevy made the Monza Spyder a separate 600 series with a bigger (but not higher horsepower) engine. Like all 1964 powerplants, this was an enlarged 163.8 ci six that had improvements to reduce oil seal leakage (a problem that plagued the earlier Corvairs). Since sales

'61 CHEVY CORVAIR: THREE TRANSMISSIONS

You know, one extremely pleasant thing about Corvair is its versatility. For instance, take transmissions. You can, of course, choose the standard three-speed box or Corvair Powerglide*.

But the big news (fanfare, please) is our new floor-mounted all synchro-mesh four-speed transmission*. Essentially, it's patterned after the design you'll find on many a Corvette—and the experts say that one's among the best in the business. For the technically minded, Corvair's four speeds line up like this: first, 3.65:1; second, 2.35:1; third, 1.44:1 and top 1.00:1. Nicely spaced, superbly supple.

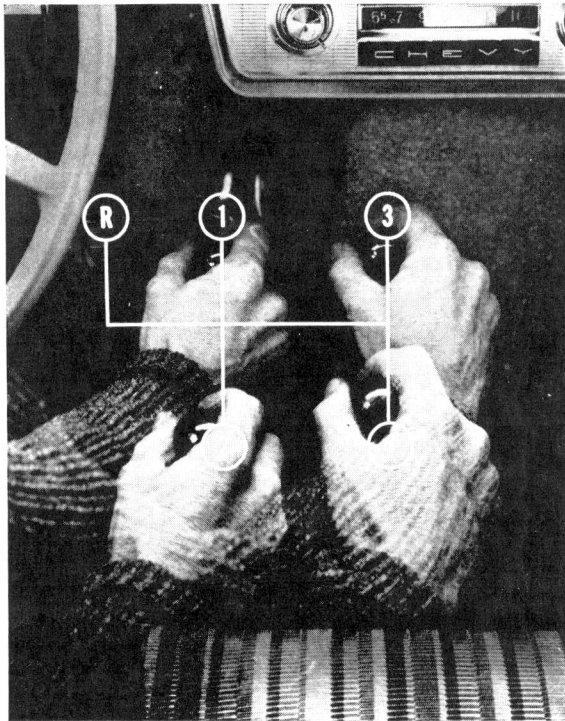

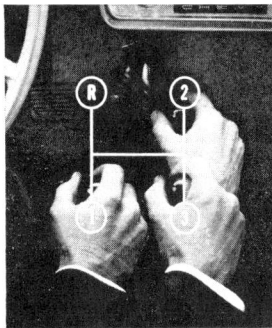

Now, maybe you figure a four-speed gearbox gives you just another gear to shift. But then maybe you've never dropped your hand onto a palmful of pure driving sport. Frankly, though, it's next to impossible to sell you on an outfit like this in words. You've got to sell yourself —which you'll probably do, once you've had a taste of it. At your Chevrolet dealer's. . . . Chevrolet Division of General Motors, Detroit 2, Michigan. *Optional at extra cost.

corvair
by Chevrolet

The lively Corvair 700 Club Coupe

Corvair, you know, is still the most advanced car in the land—and we've had a solid year to refine those engineering marvels: independent suspension all round . . . air-cooled aluminum engine in the rear and all the rest. Check into it—and while you're at your dealer's, get a load of that Greenbrier Sports Wagon!

Corvair advertisement of 1961 shows 700 series Club Coupe in profile. Transmission options— two-speed Powerglide with dash-mounted control lever or three-speed manual gearbox with floor shifter and four-on-the-floor performance option—are highlighted in the copy.

This Corvair 700 4-Door Sedan has provisions for heating ducts built right into its Body by Fisher.

More happy ideas from the new '61 CHEVY CORVAIR!

more spunk, savings and travel space!

Wasn't easy, but we managed to make Corvair even more desirable in '61: we boosted the displacement of that air-cooled rear engine to 145 cubic inches. Made Corvair even thriftier to run: Coupes and Sedans carry lower prices, and quicker cold-start warmup gets you saving fast. (There's a new heater* that distributes heat more evenly, and a longer range fuel tank.) Added space inside for you, up front for your luggage. (Sedans and Coupes give you nearly 12% more space under the hood.) You'll like Corvair's smarter styling, too, the minute you see it. But that's not the half of Corvair's good news for '61. Now Corvair has family-lovin' wagons for you! Interested? Read on!

Chevrolet Division of General Motors, Detroit 2, Michigan/ *optional at extra cost.

The Lakewood 700 Station Wagon—4 doors and up to 68 cubic feet of cargo area.

Coming your way—the nimble Greenbrier Sports Wagon.

The Lakewood Station Wagon does a man-sized job with cargo, yet handles like a charm. Our Greenbrier Sports Wagon—unlike anything ever built in America before—has space for up to 175.5 cubic feet of people and things on a maneuverable 95" wheelbase. Check that against the wagons you're used to. Same rear-engine traction, same parkability that have become a Corvair trademark. See the whole sensible lineup soon—at your Chevrolet dealer's.

Another 1961 Corvair advertisement highlighted spunky performance, economy of operation and space accommodations of the rear-engined Chevy compact. It shows a 700 sedan, top, Lakewood 700 wagon, center, and van-like Greenbrier Sports Wagon, bottom.

131

were diminishing by this time, the model line-up was cut back. In addition to Monzas, the only cars left were the Corvair 500 coupe and Corvair 700 sedan.

Although similar in appearance, the 1960-64 Corvairs can be told apart easily enough. The first-year models have a concave front end panel. This was switched to a convex

Corvair Monza 4-Door Sedan

This Monza four-door sedan showed up in 1962 Corvair ad promoting "saucy new styling accents and tasteful interior trim." Bucket seats were standard in Monza coupes, but could be ordered for sedan at extra cost.

Barney Smith is the owner of this rare 1963 Fitch Sprint Corvair. Race car driver and builder John Fitch did the conversion of this ragtop himself.

Bug screen was one of Fitch's many unique accessories. *Chris Wolfe*

132

panel in 1961, and lettering on the rear deck lid (engine cover) said Corvair instead of Chevrolet. Also, the Chevy emblem on the front was widened. The Corvair sported new hubcaps in 1962 as well as a V-shaped emblem up front, which was flanked by simulated air vents. Nameplates on the front fendersides were positioned lower, behind the front wheel openings. Front panel trim was changed again in 1963. It now consisted of a horizontal strip of brightmetal with a black-finished center. Amber color parking lamps were another new touch. Corvair lettering on the rear engine cover and front trunk lid was new for 1964 and the horizontal bar across the front was made thicker that year.

Monzas had a distinctive appearance including heavy, ribbed rocker panel moldings and special nameplates behind the front wheel openings. Spyders had crossed racing flag emblems, special wheel cover inserts and goodies like a tachometer, 120 mph speedometer and brushed metal dash insert panels. The original 1962 option even included heavy-duty suspension and sintered metallic brake pads (later deleted from the standard equipment list).

A three-speed manual gearbox was standard in Corvairs. Options for shifting included a two-speed Powerglide automatic (not available for Spyders) and a four-speed manual transmission with floor shifter. A selection of optional axle ratios was offered, with the list expanded to four choices by 1963: 3.27, 3.55, 3.89 and 3.08. Coil spring suspension was used in front, with swing axles in the rear. A variety of engine options was provided.

Cars converted into Sprints by John Fitch had this special identification nameplate added. *Chris Wolfe*

Trim arrangement behind wheel identifies this 1964 Corvair convertible as a Monza Spyder.

Options included both appearance upgrades and high-performance hardware.

Early Corvair engine numbers were stamped on the aluminum engine block near the fuel pump and oil filler tube and followed the format T 0611Z, where T=Towanda assembly plant, 06=the month of production, 11=day of production and Z=transmission (Y for manual and Z for automatic). In addition to the transmission code, other letters were used to designate high-output engines and cars with air conditioning.

Ownership

The first-generation Corvairs were comfortable little cars for front passengers, but rear seats were a tight fit. Ride quality was fair with a light load, but poor with a heavy load. Test drivers reported a slight bobbing motion of the vehicle and objectionable engine noise levels; handling was rated good. A tendency to oversteer in hard cornering became a critical problem, however, when Ralph Nader played it up in his book *Unsafe at Any Speed*. It was true Corvairs wandered a bit in heavy crosswinds. Brakes were a strong point, however. Consumer reports described performance as "adequate with the more powerful engines." It was best with manual transmissions, which were more versatile for road driving than the two-speed automatic.

Being radically engineered for a US car of its era, the Corvair became a controversial vehicle. Owner surveys showed that the Corvair's biggest problem area was in mechanical engine malfunctions. The high frequency of repairs in this category put the car on *Consumer Reports'* list of undesirable models for all years of Corvair production. The car was different and consequently received a lot of negative publicity resulting in a bad reputation. Corvair experts say, however, that "unintelligent driving" was an underlying cause of several characteristic complaints.

For example, a tendency of early models to throw off blower drive belts has been traced to owners who accelerated or decelerated too quickly. This could cause sudden, momentary loss of belt tension (slop) and loss of the drive belt. Since the engine was air cooled, loss of the blower belt often led to a fried

powerplant. Chevy fixed this problem early in the game, but rumors of belt-throwing persisted for a long time.

Drivers failing to keep engine revs sufficiently high has also been pinpointed as one cause of oil cooler failures. To operate efficiently and effectively, the oil cooler required sufficient rpm to do its job.

Early Corvairs did have one engineering flaw that was unrelated to driving habits. This was in connection with the operation of engine-air exhaust doors. The system was designed so that failure of the thermostatic control—which happened often in snowy, icy areas—would cause the doors to stay in the fully closed position. On later models, the system was revised to hold the doors in the fully open position if the thermostat stuck or froze up.

Carburetor icing was experienced with some first-generation Corvairs, and the fuel system, in general, was a black area in the 1963 models' repair history. An even bigger problem was the exhaust-heater system, which could allow unhealthy levels of carbon monoxide to build up in the car's interior. In 1972, the US Department of Transportation (DOT) urged Corvair owners to have their Direct Air heaters inspected at Chevy dealerships. A factory fix was available.

The DOT warning, by the way, was tagged on to the end of a National Highway Traffic Safety Administration (NHTSA) report that exhonerated the 1960-63 Corvairs of the charges made by Nader regarding their handling and rollover characteristics. The full report appears in *The Best of Old Cars*, No. 5. It states that DOT and NHTSA made a comprehensive study of Nader's claims, using the talents of many transportation experts. The report concluded "that the handling and stability performance of the 1960-1963 Corvair does not result in an abnormal potential for the loss of control or rollover and that its handling and stability performance is at least as good as the performance of some contemporary vehicles, both foreign and domestic." It also stated "that no safety related defect exists with respect to the handling and stability characteristics of the 1960-1963 Corvair."

Even though the US government disavowed Nader's criticisms of first-generation Corvairs, collectors and restorers of the marque may find other concerns when looking for a car to buy. For example, they will have to worry about problems caused by their natural enemy, the dreaded "tin worm." There are several areas on all Corvairs where corrosion is likely to surface, plus a couple of areas where the early models were particularly rust-prone. Here's a list of some of the frequently flakey spots.

Typical Corvair rust spots
All models
Front cross-member—check riding height, springs, suspension points

Luggage compartment—check lower front corners and inside cover pan

Engine floor pan—inspect all sheet metal panels below engine cover

Front fenders—check lower rear section; open drainholes

Cowl area—check front of windshield and dash-to-windshield area

Door posts—check hinge attachment points, look for paint blisters

Wheelwells—check wheelwells and rear end of rocker panel

Doors—check front corners and bottoms of doors

Rocker panels—check panels carefully (especially on convertibles)

Rear quarter panels—check rear corner, wheelwells and bottom

Rear exhaust grille—remove grille; check surrounding sheet metal

License plate holder—check hem flange and trim screw attaching holes

Rear shocks—check attachment points in upper frame

Dashboard—check under dash trough

Floor pan tunnel—check sides of tunnel and cover pan

Gas filler door—check filler door hinge area

1960-64 models
Front fender eyebrows—check fender panels above headlamps

Front valance panel—check for internal rust in double-walled panel

Taillamp housings—check outer taillamp housings

Battery box—check box and check drain lip above the battery

Prospects
I have rated nearly all Corvairs, except the plainest four-door sedans, on the five-star scale. Even sedans are collectible, although their values tend to stay relatively unchanged over long periods of time. The Corvair has quite a large enthusiast following, since the marque club—The Corvair Society of America (CORSA)—was formed even before the model went out of production. As a result, there are thousands of Corvair col-

This 1964 Club Coupe is a Monza, but not a Spyder. There's no Spyder script below the lower front fender emblem. Wheel covers, though similar to Spyder type, have a different center insert. *Chevrolet Motor Divison*

lectors who own every year, model and body style. The plainer models are not necessarily popular as investments, but are fun-to-drive vehicles.

In the investment market, the convertibles are the dominant force, especially those with Spyder equipment. Then come the sportier coupes—Monza Spyder and Monza. The one-year-only Monza station wagon generates some special interest and the Monza sedan is also somewhat collectible. Coupes from the 500 and 700 series drop into the low end of the collectibility scale, and the Lakewood 500 station wagon, which was also a one-year model, warrants some attention because of its rarity.

Recent auction results show selling prices of between $800 and $8,000 for various Corvairs, so you can see that the range for investors is quite wide. The $800 bought an almost perfect 1964 sedan, while the $8,000 paid for a same-year Monza Spyder convertible in similar condition. Even a fairly rough Spyder ragtop will bring $2,000-plus, and an average one can command $3,800 to $6,500. By the way, the man who bid $3,800 purchased a 1962 Spyder, which is the rarest one.

Regular Monza convertible prices have gone from a low of $1,600 to a high of $5,500 for cars in just average condition. Coupes in the same shape have sold recently for as low as $1,200; however, a 1963 Monza coupe in near-perfect shape was bought at one auction for $3,800, while a sedan from the same year and series, in next-to-perfect shape, was declared sold for $2,950. The only wagon appearing at an auction recently was a 1961 Lakewood, in average shape, that netted $1,450.

As you can tell, the Corvair market is quite an open one in which it is hard to establish any definite price trends. However, the auction results do give an idea of highs and lows, plus an overall sense that values are appreciating. The bottom line is that you can find a good car at a good price if you shop carefully.

Specifications
1960-64 Corvair

	1960	1961	1962	1963	1964
Engine	six	six	six	six	six
Displacement (ci)	139.6	144.8	144.8	144.8	163.8
Horsepower (bhp)	80	80	80	80	95
Wheelbase (in.)	108	108	108	108	108
Overall length (in.)	180	180	180	180	180
Tires (in.)	6.50×13	6.50×13	6.50×13	6.50×13	6.50×14

Engines
1960-64 Corvair

Type	Bore×stroke	Ci	C.R.	Carburetion	Hp@rpm
1960-61					
Turbo Air six	3.375×2.60	139.6	8.0	2×1V	80@4400
Sp Turbo Air	3.375×2.60	139.6	8.0	2×1V	95@4800
1962-63					
Turbo Air	3.438×2.609	144.8	8.0	2×1V	80@4400
Sp Turbo Air	3.438×2.609	144.8	9.0	2×1V	102@4400
Turbo Air	3.438×2.609	144.8	8.0	1V/Turbo	150@4400
1964					
Turbo Air	3.438×2.938	163.6	8.25	2×1V	95@3600
Turbo Air	3.438×2.938	163.6	9.25	2×1V	110@4400
Turbo Air	3.438×2.938	163.6	8.25	1V/Turbo	150@4000

Production

Model no.	Type vehicle	Production
1960		
Corvair 500		
60-0569	4d Sed	47,683
60-0527	2d Clb Cpe	14,628
Corvair 700 Deluxe		
60-0769	4d Sed	139,208
60-0727	2d Clb Cpe	36,562
Corvair Monza 900		
60-0927	2d Clb Cpe	11,926
1961		
Corvair 500		
61-0569	4d Sed	18,752
61-0527	2d Clb Cpe	16,857
61-0535	4d Sta Wag	5,591
Corvair 700 Deluxe		
61-0769	4d Sed	51,948
61-0727	2d Clb Cpe	24,786
61-0735	4d Sta Wag	20,451
Corvair Monza 900		
61-0969	4d Sed	33,745
61-0927	2d Clb Cpe	109,945
1962		
Corvair 500		
62-0527	2d Clb Cpe	16,245
Corvair 700 Deluxe		
62-0769	4d Sed	35,368
62-0727	2d Clb Cpe	18,474
62-0735	4d Sta Wag	3,716
Corvair Monza 900		
62-0969	4d Sed	48,059
62-0927	2d Clb Cpe	144,844
62-0967	Conv	13,995
62-0935	4d Sta Wag	2,362

Production

Model no.	Type vehicle	Production
1962		
Corvair Monza 600 (Spyder option)		
62-0927	2d Clb Cpe	6,894
62-0967	Conv	2,574
1963		
Corvair 500		
63-0527	2d Clb Cpe	16,680
Corvair 700 Deluxe		
63-0769	4d Sed	20,684
63-0727	2d Clb Cpe	12,378
Corvair Monza 900		
63-0969	4d Sed	31,120
63-0927	2d Clb Cpe	117,917
63-0967	Conv	36,693
Corvair 900 Monza (Spyder option)		
63-0927	2d Clb Cpe	11,627
63-0967	Conv	7,472
1964		
Corvair 500		
64-0527	2d Clb Cpe	22,968
Corvair 700 Deluxe		
64-0769	4d Sed	16,295
Corvair Monza 900		
64-0969	4d Sed	21,926
64-0927	2d Clb Cpe	88,440
64-0967	Conv	31,045
Corvair Monza Spyder 600		
64-0627	2d Clb Cpe	6,480
64-0669	Conv	4,761

Chapter 13

1965-69 Corvair

★★★★★	1965-69 Yenko Stinger hardtop (Stage III and IV)
★★★★★	1965-68 Fitch Sprint convertible
★★★★★	1969 Monza convertible
★★★★	1965-69 Yenko Stinger hardtop (Stage I and II)
★★★★	1965-68 Fitch Sprint hardtop
★★★★	1965-66 Corsa convertible
★★★	1965-68 Monza convertible
★★★	1965-66 Corsa hardtop
★★	1965-69 Monza hardtop
★	1965-67 Monza four-door hardtop sedan
★	1965-69 Corvair 500 hardtop

"As new as a new car has ever been" is how GM styling chief, the late William Mitchell, summed up the restyled 1965 Corvair. Its smooth, curvy body was designed to turn on the real enthusiast. Below the surface was a totally redesigned suspension. This design eliminated many shortcomings of the original swing-axle setup. It was patterned after the system found on 1963 Corvette Sting Rays. Like the 'vette, the new Corvair handled fantastically.

A revised model line-up and new engines greeted 1965 Corvair buyers. Two- and four-door hardtops joined the ragtop in a three-car line-up. The first two came as base-level 500s and all three were offered as Monzas. At the top of the heap was a new

Restyled second-generation Corvairs look a lot alike. Here's a 1965 Monza hardtop sedan. Wire design wheel covers were $59 extra for Monzas.

Body side moldings were extra, too. *Bill and Mary Mason*

Turbocharged 1965 Corsa convertible belongs to Nester Alicea. The turbocharged engine was a $161 option. Bumper guards were a dealer installed accessory.

Circular badge on center of rear deck lid announces addition of turbocharged engine. New rear suspension for 1965 was based on Corvette type. Dealer-added bumper guards went between taillamps.

Bucket seats were standard on 1965 Monzas and also on higher-priced Corsas like Nester Alicea's ragtop. The Corsa name appears on glovebox door. This car has the floor-shifted four-speed manual gearbox.

Corsa series including both two-door models, but not the four-door. Joining the 95 and 110 hp engines of 1964 was a new 140 hp motor with four single-barrel carburetors, plus a 180 hp turbocharged Corsa-only option.

Corvair serial numbers now had thirteen symbols located on a plate on the top face of the left-hand frame side rail behind the battery bolts. The first symbol was a numeral 1 designating Chevrolet; then came the model number. The sixth symbol was the last digit of the model year, then the assembly plant code, followed by the build sequence number

Despite their numerous appearance and technical changes, second-generation Corvairs still looked like Corvairs and continued to provide Chevy fans with economical, compact-size transportation that changed little from year to year.

The Corvair 500 and Monza series were marketed all five years. Base equipment in 500s was more comprehensive than in ear-lier bottom-line Corvairs, and included even front armrests and rubber floor mats. Monzas had front and rear armrests and carpeted floors, plus full wheel covers, rocker sill moldings, bucket seats and back-up lamps. The Corsa level added such items as an electric clock, tachometer, temperature and oil pressure gauges, door panel pockets, pinstriping and special identification badges.

Styling of the second-generation Corvairs stayed virtually unchanged from year to year. You have to look carefully at small details in order to identify the vintage of the cars.

1965 Red, horizontal front molding with Chevy badge in center; Corvair script above left-hand headlamp. Government safety features not standard yet.

1966 Padded dash, padded sun visors, back-up lamps, windshield washer, left-hand outside rearview mirror and other government-required safety equipment made standard. Front trim painted blue;

Corvair script moved from over headlamp to left-hand side of front panel.

1967 Corsa series dropped. Corvair 500s and Monzas had wider taillamp bezels; heavier interior dash padding; Powerglide shift lever had ball instead of T-handle; clear plastic window knobs; new Strato-bucket seats; and oval-shaped steering wheel.

1968 Side-marker lamps added front and rear; new padded windshield posts and larger floorshift lever knob.

1969 Amber-colored front side-marker lamps; larger rearview mirror; new coated fabric upholstery trims; headrests were mandatory.

Initially, the redesigned Corvair seemed to be a marketing success, as well as a beautifully facelifted automobile. Sales for model year 1965 jumped by 30,000 cars. However, the marketplace was also becoming crowded with American-built sports compacts like the Mustang, Barracuda, Camaro, Firebird and Cougar. Some of the folks who purchased earlier Corvairs found appealing the high-performance intermediates (GTO, SS-396, Fairlane GT) as well as so-called senior compacts like the Chevy II (Nova) and Ford Falcon or Dodge Dart. These cars stole additional sales away from the Corvair.

The Corvair market eroded quickly, starting in model year 1966, when production fell to 103,743 units, or less than half the previous season's total. By 1967, the figure was down to 27,253. From there it went to 15,399 cars in 1968 and just 6,000 in 1969, the Corvair's final season.

GM abandoned the Corvair because it was expensive to produce and had become a public relations problem. In addition, the Camaro, Chevy II and Chevelle, collectively, were in competition for many of the same buyers, so the need for the Corvair wasn't there. Some say that it was kept until 1969 to amortize tooling costs. Others felt that Chevrolet general manager Ed Cole—who played a major role in creating the Corvair— had a special place in his heart for the car. Besides that, the open feud between GM and Ralph Nader made the Corvair a symbol of victory or defeat to the watching public.

Before the Corvair faded away, several sports racing car builders began offering special equipment for both chassis and engine. As early as 1961, champion racer

This 1966 Corvair hardtop has the Monza emblem behind front wheel cutout. Front trim bar had blue-painted insert this year. *Bill and Mary Mason*

On 1966 Corsas, the model name stood out on the side of the cowl below mid-body feature-line. This was the last season for the high-performance Corvair series. *Chris Wolfe*

The 1966 Yenko Stinger was an aftermarket specialty conversion done by Chevrolet dealer Don Yenko of Canonsburg, Pennsylvania. It was intended for competition in SCCA sedan racing classes. Features included blue stripes on a white-finished body and blacked-out headlamps. *Chris Wolfe*

Andy Granatelli built a Paxton supercharged version which he drove to a record 142 mph on the Bonneville Salt Flats. Drag racer Dick Griffin developed an aluminum manifold which accommodated a Volkswagen Stromberg carburetor. EMPI, of California, offered aluminum-bronze alloy valve guides for the air-cooled engine, while Bill Thomas marketed as SS induction system with a bigger-than-stock induction tube and twin carburetors for the Spyder motor. Wallin Piper, of Santa Ana, California, set three Bonneville records with a 1965 Corsa coupe and went into custom engine building for Corvair enthusiasts.

One highly collectible aftermarket-modified Corvair is the Fitch Sprint, built by John Fitch of Connecticut, a former sports car racing champion. The first Fitch Sprints, appearing around 1963, were based on the Monza Spyder. Modifications were made to the chassis and drivetrain to help the cars run competitively in Sports Car Club of America (SCCA) sedan racing classes. A four-carburetor engine setup was available from Fitch, prior to the factory version. Fitch continued offering Sprint equipment for second-generation Corvairs, with his ultimate kit including a fiberglass extension that gave the coupe a fastback roofline.

Another specialty offering—the Yenko Stinger—was developed and sold by Don Yenko between 1965 and 1969. Starting with a Corsa coupe, Yenko Sportscars offered four engine modification packages: Stage I (160 hp); Stage II (190 hp); Stage III (220 hp); and Stage IV (240 hp). Only the most powerful of these (not available in 1969, by the way) had a larger-than-stock 176 ci displacement. The Stage II Corvair had a 10.1:1 compression ratio, while a 10.5:1 ratio was used for Stage III and Stage IV versions. Approximately 100-135 Yenko Stingers were sold in four years. The SCCA recognized these cars as production models and they are becoming quite collectible.

The 1966 Corvair-based Yenko Stinger coupe had specially modified rear quarter window treatment with rear of window opening filled-in to enhance aerodynamics. *Chris Wolfe*

Ownership

Despite the numerous product refinements, car magazines and consumer publications found the second-generation Corvairs very similar, overall, to the earlier models. *Consumer Reports* continued to classify the little Chevy as an undesirable automobile and indicated that Corvairs had low resale values. In 1969, a two-year-old Monza was worth only $1,450, or about $1,000 less than its original price. In 1971, a two-year-old Monza that sold for $2,522 new was valued at $1,675.

Surveys of service required by original owners of second-generation Corvairs indicate that the 1965 models were the most frequently repaired. They had an above-average number of problems with fuel system components, steering, engine, body (squeaks and rattles), rear axles, shock absorbers, transmission, clutch and wheel alignment. Improvements for 1966 reduced service calls for steering, engine and body repairs to about average levels. By 1967, additional refinements to the Corvair brought an obvious reduction of major service calls, but the engine, clutch and body exterior still required slightly above average attention.

The last two Corvairs were the best of the late-models as far as frequency of fixing is concerned. However, the incidence of engine repairs increased and the clutch still required more than a normal amount of service. Slightly above average exterior body repairs showed up, too. At the same time, most other systems were coming in with less than average or far less than average repairs needed. The 1969 models had even better electrical system and automatic transmission ratings, but clutch repairs took a slight jump and front suspension work orders increased, too.

All in all, in terms of original owner surveys, the number of trips back to the dealer service department decreased as the Corvair series continued in production with only minor annual changes. This may have taught GM somewhat of a lesson; it wasn't long before extensive model-year changes started to become a thing of the past. As we know, today it is next to impossible to tell a car apart from the next year's model.

As indicated and charted in the previous chapter, a typical problem that Corvair collectors face is rust spots on the unit-body structure, as well as on both the front and

Full wheel covers were standard on 1967 Monza four-door hardtop sedan. Front seats were buckets; rear seat on all models, except convertible, was of fold-down design. GM introduced five-year engine and drivetrain warranty this season.

rear stub-frame assemblies. With later models, corrosion was reduced somewhat above the headlamps, on the front valance panel, around the outer taillamps and near the battery box. There are, however, a couple of spots on 1965-69 models that became more difficult to repair once rust set in. They include the lower section of the front wheelwell (where it's spot-welded to the inner trunk panel) and the frame rail side pans (at their extreme rear). Check both of these areas carefully when inspecting these cars, since passing up a rusty vehicle may avoid the extra restoration hassles involved.

Prospects

Collector car auction results indicate that most second-generation Corvairs can be purchased in the same general price range as comparable early models. However, you must take into consideration the fact that the Spyder was no longer offered, so top-model values come in slightly lower. For instance, while a good Spyder convertible brings around $8,000, a similar-condition Corsa ragtop (even with the turbo engine) peaks at $6,900. Still, the other models—Corvair 500s and Monzas—will sell for about what the earlier versions of similar body style bring. I say *similar* body style,

because models available in the early years (club coupe and sedan) were replaced by a two-door hardtop coupe and four-door hardtop sedan after 1965. Some typical auction prices include $3,800 for a top-condition 1966 Monza convertible, $2,000 for a perfect 1965 Corvair two-door hardtop and $1,150 for a mid-range condition 1965 four-door hardtop.

An exception to the same-as-before price range picture seems to exist in the case of the 1969 Monza convertible, which has the plus factor of exceptional rarity going for it. Only 521 of these cars were manufactured, which makes them the rarest Corvair passenger cars ever built. In addition, the 1969 Monza ragtop is considered historic as the last of the Corvair line. During 1987, three of these cars were sold at specialty auctions and all three brought strong prices for the condition they were in.

The first, a next-to-perfect car, was bid to $5,000 and not sold. Then there was a fairly average example, which bid to $4,250 and also didn't sell. Last, but certainly not least, was the third car—a perfect original with only forty-two original miles—which found a new owner at $12,000! That's a world-record price for any Corvair!

Monza was the top series again in 1968, but no longer included a four-door. Still made were the convertible and Sport Coupe shown here. Front and rear side-marker lamps were new.

Decal on 1969 Corvair engine air cleaner indicates its 164 ci displacement. Spare tire was carried inside rear right-hand fender, next to engine. New emissions control equipment was phased-in for 1968 and 1969. *Tony Hossain*

When it comes to performance-converted Corvairs like the Fitch Sprint and Yenko Stinger, there are no auction results to go by. *The Standard Catalog of American Cars 1946-1975* lists a range of values between $2,700 (restorable) and $18,000 (excellent) for a Yenko Stinger, which seems to be within the realm of reality, considering the current marketplace emphasis on high-performance cars. Regardless of price, both of these conversions look like five-star investments. They are not viewed simply as modified factory cars (which might turn off a serious investor). Instead, they are seen as legitimate special-interest sports-racing cars that played a significant role in the Corvair's historical development.

Larger rearview mirror and amber-colored parking lamp lenses are clues to 1969 Corvairs. *Tony Hossain*

Specifications
1965-69 Corvair

	1965	1966	1967	1968	1969
Engine	six	six	six	six	six
Displacement (ci)	163.6	163.6	163.6	163.6	163.6
Horsepower (bhp)	95	95	95	95	95
Wheelbase (in.)	108	108	108	108	108
Overall length (in.)	183.3	184	183	183	183
Tires (in.)	6.50×13	7.00×14	7.00×13	7.00×13	7.00×13

Engines
1965-69 Corvair

Engine name	Bore×stroke	Ci	C.R.	Carburetion	Hp
1965-66					
T-A 164	3.438×2.938	163.6	8.25	2×1V	95@3600
T-A 164 Hi-Perf	3.438×2.938	163.6	9.25	2×1V	110@4400
T-A 164 Sp Hi-Perf	3.438×2.938	163.6	9.25	4×1V	140@5200
Turbocharged 164	3.438×2.938	163.6	8.25	1V/Turbo	180@4000
1967-69					
T-A 164	3.438×3.938	163.6	8.25	2×1V	95@3600
T-A 164 Hi-Perf	3.438×2.938	163.6	9.25	2×1V	110@4400
T-A 164 Sp Hi-Perf	3.438×2.938	163.6	9.25	4×1V	140@5200

Production

Model no.	Type vehicle	Production
1965		
Corvair 500		
65-10139	4d HT Sed	17,560
65-10137	2d HT Cpe	36,747
Corvair Monza		
65-10539	4d HT Sed	37,157
65-10537	2d HT Cpe	88,954
65-10567	Conv	26,466
Corvair Corsa		
65-10737	2d HT Cpe	20,291
65-10767	Conv	8,353
1966		
Corvair 500		
66-10139	4d HT Sed	8,779
66-10137	2d HT Cpe	24,045
Corvair Monza		
66-10539	4d HT Sed	12,497
66-10537	2d HT Cpe	37,605
66-10567	Conv	10,345
Corvair Corsa		
66-10737	2d HT Cpe	7,330
66-10767	Conv	3,142

Production

Model no.	Type vehicle	Production
1967		
Corvair 500		
67-10139	4d HT Sed	2,959
67-10137	2d HT Cpe	9,257
Corvair Monza		
67-10539	4d HT Sed	3,157
67-10537	2d HT Cpe	9,771
67-10567	Conv	2,109
1968		
1968 Covair 500		
68-10137	2d HT Cpe	7,206
1968 Corvair Monza		
68-10537	2d HT Cpe	6,807
68-10567	Conv	1,386
1969		
1969 Corvair 500		
69-10137	2d HT Cpe	2,762
1969 Corvair Monza		
69-10537	2d HT Cpe	2,717
69-10567	Conv	521

Chapter 14

1962-67 Chevy II and Nova

★★★★★	1966 Nova SS Sport Coupe (L-79)
★★★★	1967 Nova SS Sport Coupe (L-79)
★★★★	1963 Nova SS convertible
★★★	1963 Nova convertible
★★★	1964-65 Nova SS Sport Coupe (V-8)
★★★	1964-67 Nova station wagon (327 ci V-8)
★★	1966-67 Nova SS Sport Coupe (V-8)
★★	1963 Nova SS Sport Coupe (6-cyl)
★★	1964-67 Nova station wagon (283 ci V-8)
★★	1964-67 Nova coupe and sedan (V-8)
★	1963-67 Nova coupe and sedan (6-cyl)
★	1963-67 Nova station wagon (6-cyl)
★	1962-67 Chevy II

Chevrolet introduced a simple, boxy car for its 1962 model year. Named the Chevy II, it was intended to compete with the popular Ford Falcon as an entry-level model perfect for working women, fleet sales and young drivers. The Chevy II came in three levels of trim with a base four-cylinder engine or optional six. The fanciest model, called the Nova 400, used the six as standard equipment. The 100 and 300 series Chevy IIs were Spartan, basic transportation vehicles, while the Nova was the image car of the line.

From the beginning, Novas ran away with the bulk of sales and had the most appeal to enthusiasts. Before long, Chevy added the Nova SS option for the Sport Coupe and convertible, which were body styles exclusive to the top series. Then came an optional 283, followed by even larger V-8 powerplants, some of which made the little Chevys fly like factory hot rods.

Though the Chevy II marketing program lacked consistency, the Nova and Nova SS clearly stood out as the most exciting models. Today they are considered the collector cars of the bunch, while the plainer Chevy IIs attract little attention.

To help identify a Chevy II, check the VIN on the left door hinge pillar. The first symbol shows the last digit of the model year. It is followed by the model number, assembly plant code and a six-digit sequential production number. All Novas have 0400 series model codes and factory designations of W for Willow Run, Michigan, or N for Norwood, Ohio.

All 1962-67 Novas had the same basic specifications, except for larger tires on 1967s. Specs include a 110 in. wheelbase, 183 in. overall length, 194.4 ci 120 hp overhead-valve six as standard powerplant, and blackwall tires that were size 6.50x13 through 1966 and 6.95x14 for 1967.

Chevy IIs had somewhat unique body construction with two box-like units. One was the main body; the second, forward from the firewall, was bolted to the first. Bolt-on front fenders—designed for ease of repairs—were attached to the forward unit.

The independent front suspension had high-mounted coil springs with double-action shocks inside them. The rear suspension had single-leaf Mono-Plate springs at each wheel with diagonally mounted shocks. These Mono-Plate springs became a problem when high-performance engines were offered, as they sometimes twisted under a big V-8's torque loads.

For '62 your Chevrolet dealer's

Impala Sport Coupe

'62 Chevrolet

Built for people who want room, refinement and riding comfort found in much more expensive cars

Chevy II 300 2-Door Sedan

the new Chevy II

Built for people who want modern basic transportation in the best Chevrolet tradition. Here they are—a totally new line of thrift cars from Chevrolet, encompassing a whole new concept of engineering simplicity to clamp down on service and maintenance cost. Bolt-on front fenders, roomy engine compartment and easy accessibility of adjustable components are just a few of the maintenance advantages of Chevy II's unique design. Thrifty 4-cylinder engine (also satin-smooth 6) wrings extra miles out of a gallon of regular. Unique Mono-Plate rear springs do away with the friction and harshness of old-style springs to give you a remarkably smooth ride. These and a host of other surprises in nine spanking new-sized models, including station wagons and the soon-to-come hardtop and convertible.

Chevy II 300 two-door sedan was featured in 1962 advertisement. Bodyside moldings were included on this series, but not full wheel covers.

Superior corrosion protection was a Chevy II selling point that modern restorers still appreciate. Chevy also promoted its Safety-Master brakes, Magic-Mirror acrylic paint, high-level ventilation and a built-in blended-air heater and defroster system.

The Chevy II six featured overhead valves, aluminum pistons, a forged steel crank, hydraulic lifters, a positive shift starter, oil-wetted air cleaner and Full-Flow oil filter.

Grille revision for 1963 Chevy II eliminated horizontal center molding. Chevrolet name replaced badge on hood. Nova 400s, like Jim Schneider's six-cylinder Sport Coupe, had bodyside and rocker panel moldings, plus full wheel discs. These are optional wheel covers, however.

Last year for a Chevy II ragtop was 1963; it came only as a Nova. This example sports the standard full wheel covers and whitewall tires. *Chris Wolfe*

Three-speed synchromesh gear-shifting with a 9.12 in. diameter clutch was standard; Chevy's two-speed Powerglide automatic transmission was optional. Two radios, power steering, power brakes, air conditioning and many more extras were offered. There was a number of heavy-duty component options—clutch, springs, shocks and battery—for performance fans, plus sintered metallic brake linings. Even police car and taxicab kits were available.

Two- and four-door sedans and a four-door wagon were first offered in all car lines. Novas also came as Sport Coupes and convertibles until 1963. Both sporty models were dropped at the beginning of model year 1964, however, out of fear they would steal sales from Chevy's new Chevelle. When enthusiasts let out a howl, the Sport Coupe was revived, but the ragtop was gone permanently.

Nova 400 features included all of the following: special rear fender (or front fender some years) nameplates; bodyside, window and rear deck lid moldings; ribbed rocker sill moldings; front windsplit moldings; bright parking lamp extensions; dual sun visors; cigarette lighter; lockable glovebox; automatic interior light switches; foam seat cushions; padded front and rear armrests; built-in ashtrays; color-keyed rubber floor mats with deep-twist carpet inserts; and full wheel covers. Convertibles had a counterbalanced manual top with color-keyed fabric roofs.

Sedans and Sport Coupes featured rich, vinyl-trimmed pattern cloth upholstery, while (for 1962) wagons and ragtops featured all-vinyl seats in fawn, aqua, red, blue and gold color choices. Front bucket seats were optional in convertibles and Sport Coupes. The original (1963) Super Sport package included the bucket seats, SS emblems, wider bodyside moldings, silver anodized rear panel finish and finned wheel covers. With Powerglide, the Nova SS received a front console.

In 1963, the Nova SS was a model option; from 1964-67 it became a separate series. At first, this was primarily a cosmetic treatment, but high-performance add-ons were offered later. The one-year-only convertible left the factory with only a six-cylinder engine. After mid-1963, however, Chevy offered a service kit to dealers for V-8 engine conversions. Therefore, it's not impossible that a few convertibles were among the handful of cars delivered to buyers with dealer-installed V-8s.

Year-to-year styling revisions were minimal between 1962 and 1965. They consisted mainly of grille design and trim location changes. Significantly revised sheet metal was tailored for 1966-67 Chevy IIs, which look taller, sleeker and more slab-sided. These Novas were two inches wider and had a mild Coke-bottle shape that looked rather sporty.

1962 Grille had prominent, bright horizontal bar across center; the hood wore a Chevrolet emblem.

1963 Grille had five wider, horizontal blades with closer-spaced vertical supports behind them; Chevy front emblem moved to hood lip molding. Rear Chevy emblem had full-width extensions.

1964 Grille had a more crosshatched appearance, with a wider hood lip molding above it. Nova nameplates on front fenders.

Nova badge moved from rear fenders to front fenders in 1964. Wagons came only with sixes and V-8s starting this season. Small hubcaps are shown here. Chevy emblem returned on hood lip molding.

Nova wagon's second seat folded flat with floor for passenger-to-cargo conversion. Stowage space totaled 76.2 cubic feet with seat down; total load length with tailgate lowered was over nine feet. The 1964 Nova wagon was a six-passenger model on which a power rear window cost extra.

1965 Chevy badge in center of grille with seven narrow horizontal bars extending to headlamps; Nova script and badge on rear fenders. Novas had twin rear lamps; back-up lamps inboard.

1966 New body with taller fenders that arched over headlamps. Grille had horizontal and vertical elements and nameplate on left side. Vertical taillamps with back-up lens at bottom (except wagons).

1967 Egg-crate grille with wide horizontal center bar. Vertical taillamps had back-up lens just below center. Novas had "waffle" texture rear beauty panel with narrow Chevy II or SS emblem at right.

Ownership

Chevy IIs, in general, drew mixed reviews from car critics. Accommodations and ride quality generally were rated on the low end of the scale and the single-leaf springs were a drawback, even with normal passenger loads. Handling and steering were summed up as fair to good, as was the Safety-Master brake system. Sixes sometimes ran into problems with throttle linkage clearance, which could cause the accelerator to stick wide-open. The V-8s were much better overall. Models with Powerglide were noted for a lack of shifting versatility, though.

One of my friends drove a four-cylinder Chevy II as a salesman's car. It was cute and likable, but had no guts and broke down frequently. Sixes were much smoother, quieter and more reliable and provided adequate power. After 1964, however, the V-8 options were the way to go. *Consumer Reports* tagged the 1966-67 Chevy IIs undesirable cars, both sixes and V-8s, but they probably never tried out a high-performance model. These cars were very desirable to those who found big engines in small cars enticing.

Repairwise, the 1962 models look like the worst buys. Black spots on their service records included steering, rear axles, rust, shock absorbers, wheel alignment and body rattles and squeaks, all occurring far more than normal. However, the drivetrain required only an average number of repairs.

Rattles, squeaks and wheel alignment problems continued at an above-average rate through 1966. After 1963, service calls on rear axles tapered off to normal, so the 1964s and 1965s were pretty darn good cars. Like the 1962 models, the restyled 1966s

The 1964 Nova 100 two-door sedan was a basic-looking car with only thin rocker panel accents and small hubcaps. Badge behind front wheel is for six, which also had a Nova Six rear fender nameplate. *Chevrolet Motor Division*

INSTRUMENT CLUSTER

WHEEL DISC

NOVA EMBLEM

← REAR QUARTER
PANEL
CHEVY II 100
IDENTIFICATION

← FRONT
AND
REAR
ORNAMENTS
↓

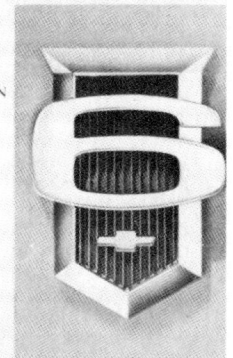

ENGINE IDENTIFICATION

Sales catalog artwork shows details for 1964 Chevy II 100 and Nova trim. Super Sports (not shown) added a badge bar on upper right corner of rear cove and bold SS emblems on front fenders just ahead of doors.

also required above-average repair work. Steering, rust and transmission problems plagued the 1966s, in addition to the typical things. However, it seems like some fast improvements were accomplished, since the 1967 models had the best frequency of repair record of all the early Chevy IIs. The fuel system was something new to worry about, though.

In the collector market, the top dogs are the Nova and Nova SS, particularly the 1966 Super Sport with the L-79 engine. These

This nicely restyled 1965 Nova SS Sport Coupe appeared at a car show in Eagle River, Wisconsin. Hood now had Chevrolet name, while grille wore Chevy emblem in center. Headlamp screens were a period accessory.

The 1965 model's taillamps were squarer shaped and mounted in the fenders. Back-up lamps had the same shape and went on the deck lid. A Chevy emblem decorated rear beauty panel, which had a Chevrolet nameplate above it.

Nova SS badges were moved to rear fender in 1965. There was similar identifying trim on the right-hand edge of the deck lid. Rear beauty panel was a distinction of all Novas.

Revisions for 1966 included an extensive face-lifting of original body that gave a taller, wider appearance. Both cars seen here have circular SS emblem alongside Nova nameplate on the left-hand side of their grilles. Car on right also has optional bumper guards and spinner wheel covers. *Chris Wolfe*

154

were excellent performance cars, especially when modifications were done to the rear suspension and fatter-than-stock tires were added. With stock springs and skinny tires, magazine test drivers got mixed results at the drag strip.

Prospects

The 1967 Novas with the L-79 option are, of course, exceptional rarities. But they're hard to come by. Consequently, the better known 1966 version is more actively sought and seems to be worth more. This is probably the best investment you could make in early Novas.

Another model collectors love is the one-year-only Nova SS convertible. This ragtop brings strong prices, even though the six-cylinder engine is used. However, these cars have to be in top condition and have lots of options to be a good investment. Parts for them are extremely hard to find and expensive; therefore, a restoration can be a costly proposition and hurt investment potential.

Other very good cars to sink money into are non-Super Sport convertibles, 1964-65 Nova SS Sport Coupes and V-8 powered station wagons. Again, for the pre-1966 models, condition is a critical factor. You rarely can restore a rough car and make the effort pay.

Nova and Nova SS models do not show up frequently at collector car auctions. Many enthusiasts find this a benefit, when it comes to purchase prices. During 1987, only twelve cars were consigned to major sales.

With the exception of the one, rare high-performance model, it looks like the normal price range for early Novas—from sedans to Sport Coupes—is in the $2,000 to $4,000 bracket. The SS models and those with the bigger V-8s will, naturally, sell at the top of the range in most cases.

New body panels and an extruded aluminum grille were among changes for the 1966 Novas. This car has the Super Sport script on rear fenders and circular SS badge on right-hand side of rear beauty panel. Wheel covers also sport SS center inserts.

These triple section taillamps were used only on Chevy II station wagons for 1967. The badge on the rear beauty panel is redesigned from 1966. The wagon was the heaviest Chevy II and came with six-cylinder and V-8 powerplants.

A wide horizontal bar was added to the center of the 1967 grille, which now had behind-the-headlamp extensions. Chevy badge at center of hood was scaled down in size. Super Sport name appears on rear fender; SS initials at left of grille. Crossed flag emblem behind front wheel cutout indicated 327 ci V-8 engine.

Engines
Chevy II and Nova

Type	Bore×stroke	Ci	Carburetion	C.R.	Hp@rpm
I-6	3.56×3.25	194	1V	8.5	120@4400
I-6	3.87×3.25	230	1V	8.5	140@4400
I-6	3.88×3.53	250	1V	8.5	155@4200
V-8	3.87×3.00	283	2V	9.25	195@4800
V-8	3.87×3.00	283	4V	10.25	220@4800
V-8	4.00×3.25	327	4V	10.50	250@4800
V-8	4.00×3.25	327	4V	10.50	300@5000
V-8	4.00×3.25	327	4V	10.50	275@4800
V-8	4.00×3.25	327	4V	11.00	325/350@5800

Performance
Nova

Year/model	Ci/Bhp	0-60 mph	¼ mile
'64 Nova SS Spt Cpe	283/195	11.3 sec	18 sec
'66 Nova SS Spt Cpe	327/275	8.6	18.4
'66 Nova SS Spt Cpe	327/350	7.2	18.0
'66 Nova SS Spt Cpe	327/350	7.2	15.1

Production

Model no.	Type vehicle	Production
1962		
Nova		
0449	4d Sed	139,004
0441	2d Sed	44,390
0437	2d Spt Cpe	59,586
0467	Conv	23,741
0435	4d Sta Wag	—
1963		
Nova		
0449	4d Sed	58,862
0437	2d Spt Cpe	87,415
0467	Conv	24,823
0435	4d Sta Wag	—

Note: A total of 42,432 Nova Sport Coupes and convertibles had the SS option in 1963.

Model no.	Type vehicle	Production
1964		
Nova		
0469	4d Sed	—
0411	2d Sed	—
0437	2d Spt Cpe	—
0435	4d Sta Wag	—
Nova SS		
0447	2d Spt Cpe	10,570

Note: Rounded off to the nearest 100 units, production of 1964 Novas (excluding station wagons) was 102,900 cars. This includes Nova SS models.

Model no.	Type vehicle	Production
1965		
Nova		
11569	4d Sed	—
11537	2d Spt Cpe	—
11535	4d Sta Wag	—

Note: Rounded off to the nearest 100 units, production of 1965 Novas (excluding station wagons) was 51,700 cars. This does not include Nova SS models.

Production

Model no.	Type vehicle	Production
Nova SS		
11737	2d Spt Cpe	9,100
1966		
Nova		
11569	4d Sed	—
11537	2d Spt Cpe	—
11535	4d Sta Wag	—

Note: Rounded off to the nearest 100 units, production of 1966 Novas (excluding station wagons and Nova SS) was 73,900 cars. This included 54,300 sixes and 19,600 V-8s. Price and weight shown for six-cylinder.

Model no.	Type vehicle	Production
Nova SS		
11737	2d Spt Cpe (6-cyl)	6,700
11837	2d Spt Cpe (V-8)	16,300

Note: Approximately 200 cars had the L-79 engine option.

Model no.	Type vehicle	Production
1967		
Nova		
11569	4d Sed	—
11537	2d Spt Cpe	—
11535	4d Sta Wag	—

Note: Rounded off to the nearest 100 units, production of 1967 Novas (excluding station wagons and Nova SS) was 47,600 cars. This includes 34,400 sixes and 13,200 V-8s. Price and weight shown for six-cylinder.

Model no.	Type vehicle	Production
Nova SS		
11737 (6-cyl)	2d Spt Cpe	1,900
11837 (V-8)	2d Spt Cpe	8,200

Note: Seven cars had the L-79 option.

Nova auction results

Year/model	Condition	High bid	Sold
1963 Nova Sport Coupe	fine	$ 3,000	no
1963 Nova four-door sedan	very good	1,950	yes
1964 Nova Sport Coupe	excellent	3,500	no
1966 Nova Sport Coupe	very good	2,600	yes
1966 Nova Sport Coupe (L-79)	excellent	10,100	yes
1966 Nova Sport Coupe	fine	3,600	yes
1966 Nova Sport Coupe	fine	4,100	no
1966 Nova Sport Coupe	fine	2,400	yes
1967 Nova coupe	very good	3,500	no
1967 Nova six	very good	3,100	no
1967 Nova Sport Coupe	very good	4,500	no
1967 Nova four-door sedan	very good	2,000	yes

Chapter 15

1968-72 Nova

★★★★★	1968 Nova SS-396 coupe (L-38)
★★★★	1968 Nova SS-396 coupe (L-34)
★★★★	1969-70 Nova SS-396 coupe (L-38)
★★★	1969-70 Nova SS-396 coupe (L-34)
★★	1969-70 Nova SS coupe (327 and 350 ci)
★	1971-72 Nova SS-350 coupe
★	1971½-72 Rally Nova coupe (V-8)

Chevy II/Nova's first major styling change came in 1968; the look lasted seven years. Appearance revisions gave the impression of a small Chevelle with a long hood, short deck configuration and thick sail panels that widened at their base and swept sleekly into the kicked-up rear fenders. Curved side glass was also introduced.

Wheelbase and overall length increased slightly. An important engineering change was a new chassis with improved front suspension. The Chevy II/Nova shared the Camaro front stub-frame, which meant it could accommodate big-block V-8s.

In 1969, only refinements were made. The series name was shortened to Nova, and there was new bodyside trim, new interiors and thirteen new colors. Also new were grilles, taillamps and twelve finish colors. The last year for a four-cylinder engine was 1970, though collectors prefer the big V-8s, which also survived through the same year. The 1971-72 models changed very little, but engine choices were limited to the sixes and small-block V-8s. The 1971s came in twelve new colors and had redesigned standard bottlecap hubcaps that looked like old-fash-

The 1968 Chevy II had a new body. This car has the Nova SS model option, which included a 350 ci 295 hp V-8; special steering wheel; hood ornament; black grille and rear deck plates; hood insulation; deck emblem; SS grille; red-stripe tires; and six-inch wheel rims. Mag spoke wheel covers cost $32 extra.

The Chevy II name was dropped in 1969 and the Nova name was used on all models. There was only one series, but buyers could order the Custom Exterior package seen on this Nova coupe. It included simulated front fender louvers, striping and bright window moldings. Bodyside moldings were another extra.

Kelly Revabek's 1969 Nova 307 coupe sports the Custom Exterior package, which cost $98 extra on two-doors. The 307 ci V-8 was now the base V-8. Headlamp shields are an aftermarket item.

ioned baby moons with Chevy bow-ties in the center. These were also used in 1972.

Nova serial numbers consisted of thirteen symbols. Through 1971, they began with a numeral 1 for Chevrolet, followed by the two-digit series code, two-digit body type code, last digit of the model year, a letter for the factory and a sequential number starting at 100001. In 1972, this was changed and the VINs consisted of a numeral 1 for Chevrolet, a single letter for series, two digits for body style, a letter designating type of engine, the last digit of the model year, a third letter for the factory and the sequential number starting at 100001. Series and body codes correspond to model numbers shown at the end of this chapter.

Early second-generation Chevy II/Novas are easier to identify at a glance. After 1970, the cars of different model years are harder to tell apart.

1968 The 1968s carried the Chevy II name on the center of the hood lip molding. The grille had horizontal bars, and taillamps were horizontal with square white back-up lenses on the inside.

1969 A Chevy emblem was put on the hood lip molding; grilles had horizontal blades with nine vertical members. Large, vertical louvers were an option for the sides of the cowl.

1970 Front parking lamps were changed to a squarer shape and the grille had a tighter grid with nineteen vertical members.

1971 The major change was the deletion of the cowl-side louvers option. Vertical bars were also added to the wraparound grille extensions in the front body corners. Amber parking lamps were new.

1972 There was a slight change in the bevel of the 1972 Nova hood and mildly redesigned front license housing. Check serial numbers for accurate identification.

Functional improvements in 1968-72 Novas were more extensive each year than were appearance changes. For 1968 they included steel inner fenders, a computer-refined ride, side-marker lamps, increased

This 1969 Nova six coupe belongs to Alan Cradie. It has the base 230 ci 140 hp six. Party Hat wheel hub covers suggest the car has disc brake package, which was $64.25 extra.

interior room, more powerful engines, bias-mounted rear shocks, cross-flow radiator, foot-operated parking brake, keyless door locking, ignition alarm, shoulder belts, energy-absorbing front seatbacks, padded windshield pillars and seatbelts for all riders.

More rugged V-8s were introduced for 1969 along with a contoured windshield header, finned front brake drums, computer-selected springs, more durable U-joints, forward-mounted door-lock buttons, standard headrests, wider inside mirror and anti-theft ignition lock, plus Turbo Hydramatic transmission.

The 1970 Novas had refined rear shock valving and spring mountings, windshield radio antennas, a transmission-controlled spark advance system, new low-profile tires and optional variable-ratio power steering system.

A larger six was made standard in 1971, along with a side terminal battery, evaporation control system, low-lead/no-lead engines, Power-Beam headlamps, softer instrument panel knobs and a new combination emission control valve.

Improvements for 1972 included upgraded seat fabrics, added bright accents, improved V-8 engine mounts and a beefed-up rear axle.

Only two basic body styles—two-door coupe and four-door sedan—were offered from 1968-72. Series was determined by engine type: four (through 1970), six or V-8. Larger-than-base-level engines, automatic and four-speed transmissions and different trim levels were considered strictly optional.

Some Nova engine options provided truly brutal performance, although their availability wasn't widely publicized. A hefty 327 ci V-8 was released in mid-1968, along with the SS-396 big-block. The latter was carried over for 1969; however, it did not appear in Nova sales catalogs, apparently to keep GM brass from getting excited. This secretive method of marketing the big-block continued in 1970, when you could still get the engine, but only through a special fleet order program.

Like engine options, Nova transmission attachments were very performance-oriented in the late-sixties but less so in the

seventies. In 1968 they included the standard three-speed, Powerglide and close-and-wide-ratio four-speeds. Turbo Hydramatic was introduced for 1969 V-8s and four-speed gearboxes came in heavy-duty and close-ratio versions. Things were about the same for 1970. In 1971, the standard three-speed was offered for all except the Nova SS model option. Sixes could be ordered with two-speed Torque-Drive automatic or with Powerglide, which was also available with standard V-8s. Turbo Hydramatic was offered with the V-8 engine only, although Super Sports with SS Turbo-Fire 350 V-8s could be ordered with a four-speed as well. The SS Turbo-Fire engine—four-barrel 350—was exclusive to that model option. However, non-SS Novas could be had with a choice of the 307 ci V-8 or two-barrel 350.

Transmission selections were cut back slightly in 1972. The six(only one was available after 1970) came with standard three-speed or optional Powerglide. The 307 ci base V-8 came with the same choices, plus Turbo Hydramatic. Two-barrel 350 ci V-8s were offered with three-speeds or the Turbo Hydramatic, while the SS-only four-barrel 350 came with either a four-speed or Turbo Hydramatic.

Cars with the Nova SS package are the focus of collector interest. In 1968, the option (priced at $210.65) was available only for the V-8 series coupe. It included a special steering wheel; hood vent ornaments; black-accented grille and rear panel; hood insulation; SS nameplates and deck emblem; red-stripe tires; 6 in. wide wheel rims; and the 350 ci 295 hp V-8. Only 234 of these cars were built with the L-34 engine (396 ci 350 hp) and 667 were equipped with the 375 hp solid lifter L-78 version of the same engine. Such cars were capable of doing the quarter-mile in fourteen seconds at over 100 mph!

For 1969 there was a ZJ-2 Custom Exterior package with extra chrome, black body sills and accent striping; it sold for $80-$100. But the Z-26 Nova SS option was the really hot number. Priced at $280.20, its ingredients were simulated hood air intakes; simulated front fender louvers; black body, grille and rear panel accents; SS emblems; F70x14 red-stripe tires; 14x7 inch wheels;

special suspension; three-speed manual gearbox; power disc brakes; bright engine accents; hood insulation; and the new 350 ci 300 hp V-8. This engine had a stronger block and improved main bearing bulkheads. The number of Super Sports made with both 396 engines in 1969 has been listed at as low as 5,262 cars in one source, although a second source indicates 7,209 were made. In any case, the total wasn't high.

Simulated front fender louvers were part of the 1970 Nova Custom Exterior package. There was also a Custom Interior option with luxury trim, bright accents, rear armrest ashtrays, carpeting, pedal trim and extra interior lamps. The Z-26 again was available with the 300 hp base engine. It now included E70x14 white-stripe tires and a choice of Turbo Hydramatic or four-speed manual transmission. The option price jumped $10.50. In addition to the Z-26, Chevy offered the L-34 Nova SS for $184.35 extra, plus the L-38 for $316. This must have been one of the best bargains ever offered in an ultra-high-performance car.

The 1971 Nova SS base engine had the same displacement as before, but horsepower was cut to 275. Other features were the same and the price was $328. Sales catalogs highlighted extras like the custom interior, Strato-bucket seats, a center console with special "V-8 instrumentation," Rally

Foam-cushioned bench seat with rich fabric and vinyl trim was used in 1970 Nova standard interior. Other features included front safety armrests, vinyl door panels and color-keyed vinyl floor covering.

Custom bench seat interior used pattern cloth and vinyl trim over extra-thick molded foam cushions. Door panel has woodgrained trim panel.

An all-vinyl Custom interior option with bench seats was also offered in 1970. Deep-twist carpets and rear seat armrests were features of Custom-trimmed 1970 Novas.

Also available for 1970 Novas at extra-cost was the all-vinyl bucket seat interior. This car has a center console, too.

162

Crosshatched grille with tight square-shaped grid and large square parking lamps were new for 1970 Nova. Double pencil-stripe whitewalls were optional. This coupe has the $98 Custom exterior option with front fender louvers and many bright accents.

wheels and a vinyl roof covering. The SS wheels were special in that they measured 14x7 inches and had special center caps and trim rings.

While buyers could not get the Turbo-Jet 396 engine in 1971, after midyear they could order a new Rally Nova that was 350 powered and set up more for handling than brutal straight-line performance. A foward-tapering full-length bodyside stripe helped

Don Shearer brought his 1971 Nova SS-350 coupe to the Jefferson, Wisconsin, car show. The SS package was $328 and the vinyl top cost $84. There was no four-cylinder Nova this season. Non-stock wheels and headlamp shields are used on Don's car.

The 1972 Novas had no changes of an obvious nature. Chevy advertised "See less of your mechanic and more of America." This coupe has Custom Exterior Package and the $82 extra vinyl top.

163

to identify this package, which was selected as Compact Car of the Year by *Motor Trend*. Coded as the YF-1 option, it also had Rally wheels, a low price tag and a 7,700 car production run.

For 1972, the Nova SS included a 200 SAE nhp Turbo-Fire 350 V-8, Turbo Hydramatic (or four-speed), special wider-than-stock Rally wheels, white-letter tires, bright hood vents, blacked-out grille and SS emblems. A sliding sunroof was one rare new option. The Rally Sport handling and cosmetic package also returned. It featured a black-accented grille, special bodyside tape stripes and remote-control Sport mirror.

Ownership

Novas of these years excelled in handling and braking and were summed up as fair when it came to passenger accommodations. Test drivers disliked its tendency to be noisy, and it had a high frequency of repairs. Both sixes and eights were above average in respect to regular service needs. In the Nova's favor, however, were its wide interior, good brakes, excellent handling and a highly efficient heater. Power steering was a strongly recommended option.

Repair histories for these models varied widely from year to year. The 1968 V-8s are probably the best of the lot, although 1969s with such engines had no really outstanding weaknesses except for cooling and minor driveline problems. In 1970, the incidence of cooling problems was lower and the overall rating for reliability was better than average among cars of this class. In 1971 and 1972, the repair rate increased to above average, with brakes, clutches, fuel systems and manual transmissions causing the most grief.

Sixes had more frequent problems with the fuel system and ignition system in 1972, giving the Nova a significantly worse than average repair history. The 1970s were far and away the best of the six-cylinder Novas, then came the 1971s. In 1969, cooling, exhaust and fuel system problems were major black spots on the Nova's record. The 1968s went back to the shop for paint, rust and rattle problems, too. In 1971, the last year for its desirable/undesirable car ratings, *Consumer Reports* put the 1968 Nova six-cylinder and 1969 Nova V-8 on its list of undesirable models. The Novas of the seventies were not included, however. It's likely some also

Two service industry magazines did a survey of mechanics who picked the 1971 Nova as the car with the least mechanical problems and the eas-

iest to service. This is the 1972 coupe with Custom exterior trim package including pinstripes and rear grille.

would have received such ratings, had these listings continued after the cars were a few years old.

As in previous chapters, I must stress that these ratings were for cars used as everyday transportation vehicles, rather than high-performance models that enthusiasts collect today. However, the high-performance Novas do seem to have specialized appeal, even now. They are Spartan, factory hot rods that offer few frills—except for a monster engine. In fact, to some degree, the SS-396 models have *too much* horsepower for the cars to handle in stock form. Drag-racing owners of Nova SS-396s often found it necessary to add traction bars and wide tires to get the necessary bite to produce surface adhesion; therefore, a lot of the cars have numerous performance modifications added to them. Young Nova fans seem to prefer such equipment on their cars, thus it's hard to predict if a sizable market for stock-condition examples will really develop. Chances are, the hot-rod Novas will remain a specialty item with a small, but fervant following in the collector car field.

Prospects

These cars are not commonly seen at collector car auctions. Those that have shown up lately are mostly 1970-72 non-SS models in average good shape. They appear to bring prices in the $2,500 to $3,500 range. However, one SS-396 coupe in perfect condition recently was bid to $9,800 against a steeper reserve. So, the rarer Novas do bring much higher prices when they show up at the right sales.

Engines
1968-72 Nova and Nova SS

Type	Bore×stroke	Ci	CR	Carburetion	Hp@rpm
1968					
I4	3.875×3.25	153	8.5	1V	90@4000
I6	3.875×3.25	230	8.5	1V	140@4400
I6	3.875×3.53	250	8.5	1V	155@4200
V-8	3.875×3.25	307	9.0	2V	200@4600
V-8	4.001×3.25	327	10.0	4V	275@4800
V-8	4.001×3.48	350	10.25	4V	295@4800
V-8	4.001×3.25	327	11.0	4V	325@5600
V-8	4.094×3.76	396	10.25	4V	350@5200
V-8	4.094×3.76	396	11.0	4V	375@5600
1969					
I-4	3.875×3.25	153	8.5	1V	90@4000
I-6	3.875×3.25	230	8.5	1V	140@4400
I-6	3.875×3.53	250	8.5	1V	155@4200
V-8	3.875×3.25	307	9.0	2V	200@4600
V-8	4.001×3.48	350	9.0	4V	255@4800
V-8	4.001×3.48	350	10.25	4V	300@4800
V-8	4.094×3.76	396	10.25	4V	350@5200
V-8	4.094×3.76	396	11.0	4V	375@5600
1970					
I-4	3.875×3.25	153	8.5	1V	90@4000
I-6	3.875×3.25	230	8.5	1V	140@4400
I-6	3.875×3.53	250	8.5	1V	155@4200
V-8	3.875×3.25	307	9.0	2V	200@4600
V-8	4.001×3.48	350	9.0	4V	250@4800
V-8	4.001×3.48	350	10.25	4V	300@4800
V-8	4.094×3.76	396	10.25	4V	350@5200
V-8	4.094×3.76	396	11.0	4V	375@5600

Engines
1968-72 Nova and Nova SS

Type	Bore×stroke	Ci	CR	Carburetion	Hp@rpm
1971-72					
I-6	3.875×3.53	250	8.5	1V	145@4400
V-8	3.875×3.25	307	8.5	2V	200@4600
V-8	4.001×3.48	350	8.5	2V	245@4800
V-8	4.001×3.48	350	8.5	4V	270@4800

Performance
1968-72 Nova SS

Year/model	Engine	0-60 mph	¼ mile
1968 Nova SS coupe	327/325	8.7 sec	16.5 sec
1968 Nova SS coupe	396/375	6.0	14.0
1971 Nova SS coupe	350/275	8.5	15.9
1972 Nova SS coupe	350/200 nhp	8.1	15.42

Production

Model no.	Type vehicle	Production
1968		
1968 Nova V-8		
11469	4d Sed	—
11427	2d Sed	—
11427/L-48	2d SS Sed	5,571

Note: *Rounded off to the nearest 100, total production of 1968 Nova V-8s was 53,400 (including SS option production).*

Model no.	Type vehicle	Production
1969		
1969 Nova V-8		
11469	4d Sed	—
11427	2d Sed	—
11427/Z-26	2d SS Sed	17,654

Note: *Rouded off to the nearest 100, total production of 1969 Nova V-8s was 88,400 (including SS option production).*

Production

Model no.	Type vehicle	Production
1970		
1970 Nova V-8		
11469	4d Sed	—
11427	2d Sed	—
11427/Z-26	2d SS Sed	19,558

Note: *Rounded off to the nearest 100, total production of 1970 Nova V-8s was 139,243 (including SS option shown).*

Model no.	Type vehicle	Production
1971		
1971 Nova V-8		
11369	4d Sed	22,606
11327	2d Sed	70,329
11327/Z-26	2d SS Sed	7,015
1972		
1972 Nova V-8		
1X69	4d Sed	46,489
1X27	2d Sed	151,166
1X27/Z-26	2d SS Sed	12,309

Chapter 16

1970-72 Monte Carlo

★★★★★	1970 Monte Carlo SS-454 Sport Coupe (LS-6)
★★★★	1970-71 Monte Carlo SS-454 Sport Coupe (Z-20)
★★★	1972 Monte Carlo Sport Coupe (454 ci V-8)
★★	1970-72 Monte Carlo Sport Coupe (400 and 402 ci V-8)
★	1970-72 Monte Carlo Sport Coupe (350 ci V-8)

An early Chevrolet Monte Carlo might be an excellent car to buy as an investment right now. As the seventies dawned, Chevrolets were becoming quite fancy and this new model was aimed at the sports luxury market's personal-size car class. The competition included the Ford Thunderbird, Oldsmobile Toronado, Buick Riviera and Pontiac Grand Prix.

Like the Grand Prix that sired it, the Monte Carlo was based on the GM A-body Sport Coupe platform with a wheelbase extension. Like other cars in this class, it had all the things collectors love: distinctive styling, rich interior appointments, plenty of options and big V-8 engines. Although popular with those who know about it, the Monte Carlo is just starting to gain a wide following, therefore there are still good buys around.

Serial numbers for Monte Carlos follow the same system used on other 1970-71 and 1972 Chevrolets, with a total of thirteen symbols in the VIN and with a new body style and engine code system starting in 1972. The series code was the numerals 38 the first two years, but changed to a letter H in 1972. The body style code for all Monte Carlos was 57.

The new for 1970 Monte Carlo had longest hood in Chevrolet history. Car was designed to combine action and elegance in a sporty, personal luxury package. Vinyl top cost $126 extra and came in black, blue, dark gold, green or white.

In keeping with its smart new exterior, the 1970 Monte Carlo had many rich interior appointments and an optional seatback latch which unlocked folding seatbacks whenever the door was opened.

New die-cast horizontal bar grille and stand-up hood ornament identify 1971 Monte Carlo. Wheels and tires were balanced at factory for longer tread life. These are optional deluxe wheel covers. Fender skirts and vinyl top were extras, too.

Overall styling for the series' first three years was generally similar, although the grilles were totally distinctive and more brightwork was added each season. An SS-454 option was offered in 1970-71 and has become highly desirable.

1970 The grille had a mesh-style cross-hatch with chrome moldings dividing it into three horizontal tiers; hood ornament had small, fin-like design. Large, round parking lamps appeared in the front bumper.

1971 The grille had a pattern of many fine horizontal bars; stand-up hood ornament was added. Parking lamps in the front bumper were horizontally positioned rectangles.

1972 The grille had an egg-crate design, and new, vertically mounted rectangular parking lamps (the bumper was solid) flanked grille on either side. Chevy went back to a smaller, fin-like hood ornament similar to the 1970 design. At the rear, a bright horizontal decorative panel was added below the deck lid.

Monte Carlos shared the same windshield, upper roof panel and rear window used by Chevelles, so proportions of the two cars were similar. However, the front sheet metal was longer on Monte Carlos (the longest hood in Chevy's history) and wide sail panels of formal design gave it a distinctive look.

The stretched Monte Carlo platform gave it four extra inches of length ahead of the cowl, which explained the long hood and front fenders. Slab-sides and razor-edge feature-lines characterized the body. The total image was clean and uncluttered—especially in 1970—with enough bright accents to make it seem special. Fender skirts were a popular accessory, but were not used on Super-Sport-optioned cars.

Upholstery choices included a cloth and vinyl standard interior with bench seats. Strato-bucket seats in vinyl with pleated

Parking lamps moved from bumper in 1972 and stand-up hood ornament vanished. New classic precision-cast grille was seen. Rear fender skirts could be ordered for all but the SS-454 at extra cost.

170

custom-knit seating areas were available at extra cost. Another option was all-vinyl Strato-buckets. The Chevelle SS dashboard was used, but was cleverly disguised by adding simulated wood burl instrument panel inserts. Wood burl inserts also decorated the cushioned steering wheel, which had four spokes in Super Sports and two in other models. There was carpeting on the floor and bottoms, plus door panel map pockets and assist straps.

Other standard equipment included hideaway wipers; black-accented lower body and fender moldings; full wheel covers (except SS-454); power disc/drum brakes; anti-theft steering column lock; Astro-Ventilation; side-guard door beams; electric clock; protective inner fenders; forward door locks; flush-and-dry rocker panels; and a Delco Weather-Eye side terminal battery.

Regular production option Z-20 was the SS-454 package. This was required if a buyer wanted to get the 360 hp big-block engine. It also included SS-454 lettering for the rocker panels and rear deck lid; a remote-control Sport mirror; thin black stripes along the rocker panels; heavy-duty battery; dual exhausts with square-tipped chrome extensions; rear air shocks; Automatic Level Control suspension; 15x7 inch Rally wheels; and G70x15B white-stripe tires. Also included for 1971 was a blacked-out rear panel with thin accent moldings; special rear bumper with resilient insert (apparently not used on all SS-454s); heavy-duty suspension with front and rear stabilizer bars; and dash control knobs showing international identification symbols.

According to sales catalogs, only the one engine—attached to a Turbo Hydramatic transmission—was available for (and exclusive to) the 1970 Monte Carlo SS-454. At least ten cars were built with the Chevelle's LS-6 engine, however, and a handful of Monte Carlos left the factory with four-speed manual gearboxes as a special production option.

Regularly cataloged options for all Monte Carlos that are sought by collectors include a four-way power seat; AM/FM stereo tape system; power windows, door locks and trunk release; special instrumentation (with tachometer and all gauges); cruise control; tilt steering wheel; center console (with bucket seats and optional transmissions); and vinyl top.

Non-SS Monte Carlos offered a 350 ci 300 hp four-barrel V-8, a 400 ci 265 bhp four-barrel V-8 and a 402 ci 330 bhp four-barrel V-8 in 1970. The following year, the base two-barrel engine lost five horsepower and the four-barrel version of the 350 ci V-8 went to 270 bhp. Also available was a Turbo-Jet 400 ci V-8 (actually the 402 ci version of the 396 mentioned in the Chevelle section) which was rated at 300 bhp.

Since the car industry was anticipating a change to the new SAE net horsepower rating system, Chevy also listed the net horsepower ratings for the 1971 engines.

Interestingly, though all of the other engines were lower in gross horsepower (bhp), the SS-454 powerplant had a slight increase to 365 bhp. In addition, the LS-6 was again offered on a special-order basis, although not shown in sales catalogs. It was de-tuned to 425 bhp and installed in relatively few 1971 Monte Carlos.

For 1972, all engines were rated in SAE net horsepower. The options were the base two-barrel 350 ci, a 350 ci 175 nhp four-barrel, the Turbo-Jet 400 ci with 240 nhp and the Turbo-Jet 454 ci V-8 with 270 nhp. The last engine then could be ordered for all Monte Carlos and no longer came in a package including special SS equipment and identification.

Three-speed manual transmission was standard in Monte Carlos, except SS-454s. A choice of Powerglide or Turbo Hydramatic options was offered with the base 350 ci V-8. The four-barrel 350 ci engine and the 400 and 402 ci engines came with Turbo Hydramatic or four-speed options, while the 454 ci V-8 only came with Turbo Hydramatic, except for a handful of specially optioned 1970 and 1971 models.

Zero-to-60 mph with the SS-454 took around 7.7 seconds and *Car Life* magazine achieved a 16.2 second quarter-mile going over 90 mph through the traps. That was good, but not good enough in the early seventies, when true high-performance cars were at their peak in terms of go-power. So, the Monte Carlo didn't catch on with the drag-racing set.

On the other hand, the big-engined Montes proved to be extremely well suited for stock car racing, especially on short-tracks where their balance of size, weight, wheelbase and handling characteristics paid off in checkered flags. From 1971 to 1979, Chevys took ninety-eight wins in NASCAR competition. Most victories went to Monte Carlos with drivers like Richard Petty and Bobby Allison behind the wheel.

Off the tracks and on the highway, all Monte Carlos were great cruisers. Turbo-Jet-engined models could barrel across country all day long at over 110 mph speeds with no strain. That was fast enough for most owners who loved the combination of sporty good looks, personal size, above-average highway performance and luxury-level appointments. In fact, many people appreciated their Monte Carlos so much that they hung on to them for years. Enthusiasts seem to feel the same way today. Many who collect older models use their Montes for traveling to car shows—sometimes towing their vintage Chevys behind them.

Ownership

Consumer magazines rating Monte Carlos for new and used car buyers were often critical of passenger accommodations, which they found very cramped in such a big intermediate. However, they also found the model fairly smooth and quiet-riding, with engine and steering responsive to driver demands. Reduced rear visibility with the wide sail panels was a frequent complaint, plus the "floaty" ride on cars with standard suspension. Some workmanship problems (particularly door and window alignment) plagued 1970-71 models, but the 1972s were improved. Fuel economy was not good though; the two-barrel engine got only 14 mpg. The four-barrel option pulled this down to 13.5 mpg. The 402 ci V-8 was good for 13 mpg tops, and fuel usage in SS-454s and 454 powered 1972 models was in the 11-12 mpg neighborhood.

For 1972, a rear beauty panel was added to the Monte Carlo above the rear bumper. The original crest-type trunk lock cover was replaced with a small, circular chrome disc. Back-up lamps were among standard accident protec-tion features. Also included were front and rear side-marker lamps that were cleverly placed between the body perimeter molding extensions in an unobtrusive manner.

Regarding frequency of repairs, some magazines picked the 1972s as the best of the three model years, while owner surveys seem to indicate that the 1971 actually had the least service calls, statistically speaking. In 1970, cooling was a problem. Paint and overall body integrity troubled owners of 1971s and 1972s to some degree. Brakes were better than average for all years, as was the 1970-71 engine. In fact, the 1970s needed *far* less exhaust system service than typical, and the fuel and ignition systems were strong points of the 1971 models. Overall, repair needs were about average and there were (as far as my sources show) no factory recalls.

Prospects

Chevy expert (and Monte Carlo owner) Terry Boyce has suggested that these cars have a small, but deeply dedicated group of supporters in the collector car marketplace. Boyce believes that articles published in collecting magazines around 1980 made the cars better known to investors and sent the prices of SS-454s soaring. Apparently, non-SS models are entering the same cycle now. Boyce has also hinted that high asking prices might be based on this hard-core enthusiasm. He feels that actual sales are often clinched at dollar levels below those requested in advertisements.

Recent auction prices for 1970-72 Monte Carlos seem to vary. At one sale, an average good-condition 1970 base model was sold for $1,800. At another, a 1970 SS-454 in similar shape took a high bid of $3,200. However, two 1970 SS-454s in a condition one grade higher were declared actual sales at $5,850 and $7,400, respectively. In addition, a top-condition 1970 SS-454 at another sale was bid to $9,000 against the owner's even steeper reserve.

Three 1971 Monte Carlos crossed the block in 1987 auctions of record. Two were SS-454s in next-to-top shape. They drew bids of $4,250 and $4,300, but did not change hands. The third car—a non-SS model in the same condition—was a no-sale at $1,800.

Also consigned to 1987 auctions were five 1972 Monte Carlos. The first, in next-to-top shape, was a no-sale at $1,750. Two others, in average shape, were sold for $2,500 and $3,000, while another pair in similar condition were no-sales at $3,000 and $3,500.

The bottom line is that you can probably get a pretty good base model for under $3,000 and a pretty good Super Sport for about $1,000 more. However, you'll probably see a couple of five-figure asking prices for SS-454s while you're shopping, and you might have to pay that much for a good one if you wait too long.

Specifications
1970-72 Monte Carlo

	1970	1971	1972
Engine	ohv V-8	ohv V-8	ohv V-8
Displacement (ci)	350	350	350
Horsepower (bhp or nhp)	250 bhp	245 bhp	145 nhp
Wheelbase (in.)	116	116	116
Overall length (in.)	206	207	207
Tires (in.)	G78×15	G78×15	G78×15

Engines
Monte Carlo

Ci	Carburetion	SAE nhp	Std/opt
350	2V	165	std
350	4V	175	opt (not in SS-454)
400 (402)	4V	260	opt (not in SS-454)
454	4V	285	std (SS-454 only)

Production

Model no.	Type vehicle	Production
1970 Monte Carlo		
13857	2d HT	126,844
13857/Z-20	2d SS-454 HT	3,823

Note: Total production (all model options) was 130,657 units in 1970. About 10 of the SS-454 Monte Carlos had the LS-6 engine in 1970.

1971 Monte Carlo		
13857	2d HT	128,600
13857/Z-20	2d SS-454 HT	1.919

Note: Total production (all model options) was 128,600 units in 1971. A handful of 1971 Monte Carlo SS-454s had the LS-6 option.

1972 Monte Carlo		
1H57	2d HT	180,819

Chevrolet marque clubs

Chevrolet, general clubs
Vintage Chevrolet Club of America
PO Box 5387
Orange, CA 92667

The Chevy Association
Box 172
Elwood, IL 60421

Chevrolet, 1953-54
National Chevy Association
947 Arcade St.
St. Paul, MN 55106

Chevrolet, 1955-57
Classic Chevy International
PO Box 607188
Orlando, FL 32860

Tri Chevy Association
431 Caldwell
Chicago Heights, IL 60411

1955-1957 Chevy Owners Association
157 Coram, Mt. Sanai Rd.
Corham, NY 11727

Chevrolet, 1958-72
Late-Great Chevys (1958-64)
PO Box 607824
Orlando, FL 32860

National Impala Association
PO Box 968
Spearfish, SD 57783

1965-1966 Full-Size Chevy Club
126 Charles Rd.
Southampton, PA 18966

National 409 Chevy Club
2510 East 14th St.
Long Beach, CA 90804

Chevelle clubs
National Chevelle Owners Association
PO Box 5014
Greensboro, NC 27435

Chevy II/Nova club
National Nostalgic Nova Club
PO Box 2344
York, PA 17405

Corvair club
Corvair Society of America
2506 Gross Point Rd.
Evanston, IL 60201

To obtain information about joining a club, write to the organization and include a self-addressed stamped envelope for a reply.
Many of these clubs include local chapters in various parts of the country.

Suggested reading

Reference sources
Hundreds of books have been published about Chevrolet-built automobiles or about the eras in which postwar Chevrolets were built. It would be impossible to list all of the titles available in this space. The following are some of the titles that I referred to over and over again in compiling information for this book.

75 Years of Chevrolet
George H. Dammann
Crestline Publishing Co.
Sarasota, FL

Chevy V-8s: Enthusiasts' Guide & History 1955-1986
Terry V. Boyce
Dragonwyck Publishing Ltd.
Contoocook, NH

High-Performance Chevrolets
Richard M. Langworth
Consumer Guide
Skokie, IL

Muscle Cars
Phil Hall
Consumer Guide
Skokie, IL

The Complete Chevrolet Book, 4th edition
Peterson Publishing Co.
Los Angeles, CA

Corvair: A History & Restoration Guide
Bill Artzberger
Aztex Books
Tucson, AZ

The Hot One: Chevrolet 1955-1957
Pat Chappell
Dragonwyck Publishing Ltd.
Contoocook, NH

The Standard Catalog of American Cars 1946-1975
John A. Gunnell, editor
Krause Publications
Iola, WI